The Christian Girl's Guide to ME

The Quiz Book

D1008127

LEGACY PRESS
www.LegacyPressKids.com

The Christian Girl's Guide to ME

ME

The Quiz Book

Katrina Cassel

༄ Dedication ༄

To Jessica, Deshele, Tera, Erica, Jasmine, Tyease, Ashley, Kayla R, Chelsey, Katelyn and Kayla F—the girls who have been my daughters, whether for a few days, months, or for a lifetime. You are all precious in God's eyes!

Thank you to the many girls who tested the quizzes and gave me their thoughts. Thank you also to:
>Rick: Best friend and guide
>Tyler: Firstborn
>Jessica: Firstborn princess
>Adam: Warrior in the making
>Jasmine: My joy and song
>Kaleb and Kayla: Chosen ones
>Teresa for her valuable input, and to the Legacy team who brings the Christian Girl's Guides to life.

THE CHRISTIAN GIRL'S GUIDE TO ME: THE QUIZ BOOK
©2012 by Katrina Cassel, first printing
ISBN 10: 1-58411-087-2
ISBN 13: 978-1-58411-087-3
Legacy reorder#: LP48218
JUVENILE NONFICTION / Religion / Christianity / Christian Life

Legacy Press
P.O. Box 261129
San Diego, CA 92196
www.LegacyPressKids.com

MIX
Paper from
responsible sources
FSC
www.fsc.org **FSC® C048831**

Cover and Interior Illustrator: Shelley Dieterichs

Scriptures are from the Holy Bible: New International Version (North American Edition), ©1973, 1978, 1984, 2011 by the International Bible Society. Used by permission of Zondervan Bible Publishers.

Clue and Monopoly are registered trademarks of Parker Brothers. Family Feud is a registered trademark of Mark Goodson and Bill Todman. Pictionary is a registered trademark of Seattle Games, Inc. Stratego is a registered trademark of Milton Bradley. Twister and Scrabble are registered trademarks of Hasbro Games. LEGO is a registered trademark of Lego Group. Rice Krispies is a registered trademark of Kellogg's. Lucky Charms, Trix and Cheerios are registered trademarks of General Mills. Frisbee is a registered trademark of Wham-o.

Printed in the United States of America

Table of Contents

Introduction

Hi! Welcome to **The Christian Girl's Guide to Me: The Quiz Book.** This book is designed to help you learn more about yourself and about God. Some of the quizzes are serious and will make you think about your feelings, beliefs, strengths, and weaknesses. They'll give you tips to help you in your daily life. Other quizzes are just for fun—but you can learn more about yourself and God from them, too.

The Bible says, *"And Jesus grew in wisdom and stature, and in favor with God and man."* **(Luke 2:52)** That verse tells us that Jesus grew in four different ways.

 Jesus Grew in Wisdom. That means he grew in brainpower (mentally). Jesus got wiser and learned more and more as he grew older.

 Jesus Grew in Stature. That means he grew taller and stronger (physically). Even though Jesus was the Son of God, he still had a physical body here on Earth.

 Jesus also Grew in Favor with God. That means he grew in knowledge of God and God's laws (spiritually). Jesus learned the scriptures. He learned the importance of taking time to talk to God.

7

And, finally, **Jesus Grew in Favor with Others.**
That means he grew in knowledge of other people around
him (socially and emotionally). He
learned to get along with other
people. He learned how to act in
different situations.

There are quizzes in this book
from each of those categories.
Quizzes about God and the Bible will
have a picture of a Bible by the title.
Quizzes about brainpower will have a
picture of a scholar's hat beside the title. Quizzes about your body power
will have a picture of jogging shoes beside the title. And quizzes about
yourself and others will include the picture of a girl beside the title.

Sometimes you might be taking a quiz and none of the answers seem
to describe you. Or they might be about something you've never done.
That's okay. **You are a unique creation of God.** It would be
impossible to list all of the answers that might describe different girls.
And not all girls have had the same experiences. Just pick the
answer that sounds most like you or like what you would
do in that situation. The important thing is to learn more
about yourself and God, and to have fun doing it.

Grab a pencil and let's get started!

Quiz #1

Are You for Real?

Anyone who listens to the Word but does not do what it says is like a man who looks at his face in a mirror and, after looking at himself, goes away and immediately forgets what he looks like.

~James 1:23-24

Samantha turned off her alarm clock, and got out of bed. She walked down the hall toward the bathroom. Her brother, Justin, was just getting out of bed too. He turned to look at her. "Scary," he said.

"What's scary?" Samantha asked.

"Just take a look at yourself in the mirror," Justin said, following her.

Samantha went into the bathroom and slammed the door behind her. She looked at herself in the mirror. Samantha laughed. For once, Justin wasn't exaggerating. Samantha's hair stood up all over and her eyes were still half closed. Good thing there was time for a shower before school!

Quiz type: Spiritual

God tells us that we shouldn't just hear His Word but we should live it out. That means we need to practice our faith every day. Do you live your faith? Are you the real thing? Take the quiz below to find out. Read each situation. Then decide whether that's what you would do, what you might do, or what you would never do. Circle the best answer.

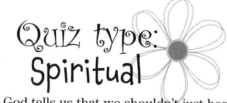

1 You plan to read your Bible before you go to bed, but by the time you get home from shopping with your mom you're really tired. You think about putting it off until the next day, but change your mind and read your Bible even though you're tired.

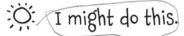 This is what I would do.

I might do this.

No way would I do this.

2 A friend asks you to pray for her grandmother. You know if you don't write it down you'll forget, so you write down the prayer request and pray for it each day.

 This is what I would do.

I might do this.

No way would I do this.

3 You hear that one of your friends said something about you that isn't true. You want to say some mean stuff about her, too. But you decide that you should talk to her and ask her if she really said untrue things about you and talk it out.

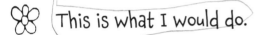 This is what I would do.

I might do this.

No way would I do this.

A girl is sitting alone at lunch. You feel bad for her because she's always alone. You have so much fun sitting with your friends. You decide to ask her to join you so she can meet your friends and have fun at lunch, too.

❀ This is what I would do.

☀ I might do this.

🐱 No way would I do this.

5 Your family is on the way home from your grandma's house Saturday night when your car has a flat tire. You get home really late so your dad says you can skip church the next day if you want. You tell him it's okay, you can catch up on your sleep later.

❀ This is what I would do.

☀ I might do this.

🐱 No way would I do this.

Which sentence did you circle the most? ☀

❀ IF YOU CIRCLED "THIS IS WHAT I WOULD DO" THE MOST—and you were honest about it—you're right on target. Your faith is real to you and you live it every day.

☀ **IF YOU CIRCLED "I MIGHT DO THIS" THE MOST,** you're in a great position to start putting your faith in action. Stop and think of some ways you can let the love of Jesus shine through you. Maybe you can invite someone to sit with you at lunch. Or offer to help a student with math. Write down some ideas and try them out.

🐱 **IF YOU CIRCLED "NO WAY WOULD I DO THIS" THE MOST,** you may want to think more seriously about the feelings of those around you. What kinds of things do you do for those you care about? When you talk with others, remember to always let Jesus' love shine through you. Ask God to help you put your faith into action. Look for ways to reach out and help others at school, in your neighborhood and at home this week.

HAVE YOU EVER LOOKED IN THE MIRROR? Of course you have! You probably look in the mirror every morning to check your hair and face before going to school, church, or out with friends. What would you do if you see crumbs on your face or notice that your hair isn't combed? Do you just walk away and forget about it? No. You fix it.

God's Word is like a mirror. When you read it, you see things that need to be fixed in your life. You might see that you aren't as kind as God wants you to be. You might find that you need to

be more honest or help more at home. If you just forget what you learn from the Bible, it's like seeing messy hair in the mirror and doing nothing about it.

Even if you don't fix the problem, and forget what you look like, others don't. And God doesn't either. Use God's mirror to help you have a beautiful heart and live out your faith.

 Find the book of James or 1 John in your Bible. They are in the New Testament. Read 10 verses in your choice of the two books every day until you have read the whole book. Find one topic in each verse that motivates you to do something. Then try to do it. Keep track of what you read for whole week. Be a doer of the Word!

Example:

1 John 1:1-2:1   *Remember to confess sin daily*

Day	Verses Read	What I did
1		
2		
3		
4		
5		
6		
7		

Phone Puzzle

God knew all about you before you were ever born. He knew your personality, your talents, and what he has planned for your future. Decode the verse below using your phone. There are two numbers under each line. The first number tells you which button to find on the phone. The second number tells you which letter. For example, the first blank is 2.2. The first 2 tells you to find the phone button with a 2 on it. The second number 2 tells you to use the second letter, which is B. So write B above the first line. For the answer, look up Jeremiah 1:5.

— — — — — —   —   — — — — — —
2.2 3.2 3.3 6.3 7.3 3.2   4.3   3.3 6.3 7.3 6.1 3.2 3.1

— — —   — —   — — —   — — — —   —
9.3 6.3 8.2   4.3 6.2   8.1 4.2 3.2   9.1 6.3 6.1 2.2   4.3

— — — —   — — —,   — — — — — —
5.2 6.2 3.2 9.1   9.3 6.3 8.2   2.2 3.2 3.3 6.3 7.3 3.2

— — —   — — — —   — — — —   —   — — —
9.3 6.3 8.2   9.1 3.2 7.3 3.2   2.2 6.3 7.3 6.2   4.3   7.4 3.2 8.1

— — —   — — — — —.   *~Jeremiah 1:5*
9.3 6.3 8.2   2.1 7.1 2.1 7.3 8.1   Puzzle answer at the end of the book.

15

What job did God have planned for Jeremiah before he was even born?

_____

_____

_____

What job might God have chosen for you before you were born?

_____

_____

_____

_____

Quiz #2

How Honest Are You?

The integrity of the upright guides them.

~Proverbs 11:3

Abby looked at the science test her teacher had just placed on her desk. She'd gotten an 88! That was much better than she'd expected. Abby quickly looked through the pages to see what she'd missed.

Abby had missed one question on the first page and two questions on the second page, but she'd missed all four questions on the back. Abby knew that each question was worth four points. The teacher must have forgotten to count the four questions on the back. She'd actually only earned a 72.

Abby sat her test back down, wishing she'd actually earned an 88. Did she really need to point out the mistake to her teacher? After all, it was *his* mistake, not hers. Abby shoved the test into her desk and tried to forget about it, but she knew her conscience would bother her if she just ignored the problem.

Abby took the test to the teacher after class and showed him the error. She hoped he'd say, "No problem, it was my mistake," but instead, he crossed out the 88 and wrote a big red 72 on the top of the test.

Abby was glad she didn't have the test grade on her conscience, but she was sad she'd done so poorly. She determined she'd study harder for the next test so she'd really have an 88—or even higher.

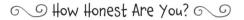

Quiz type: social/Emotional

God wants us to be honest all the time, not just when someone is watching or listening. Honesty in little things is as important as honesty in big things. Just how honest are you? Take the quiz below to find out. Circle the answer that sounds the most like what you would do in each situation.

1. You're at the fair. You have just enough money to get in and buy a wristband for all the rides, but you'll have nothing left for snacks. When you count your change later, you realize the lady only charged you the children's price and you're a year too old. **You:**

A. Keep the money. It's been a half-hour since you paid and she probably won't even remember you if you do give it back.

B. Put the money in the offering plate. It's too late to return it, but you won't be keeping it either.

C. Take the money back and explain what happened. It's not too late to do the right thing.

2 You're stuck on the third word on the spelling quiz. You just can't remember it. You glance over at your friend and accidentally see her test. You:

A. Write the word down. She should have had her test covered. You didn't mean to cheat.

B. Wait until the end of the test and write the word down if you still remember it.

C. Leave number three blank. You didn't know the word before looking around.

3 You ask to go out and play. Your mom asks if you did your math homework already. Your math is done, but you still have history homework. You:

A. Tell her that you have history homework to do.

B. Tell her that your math is done and go out and play.

C. Shrug. That way you haven't really given an answer.

4 You don't clean your room, so your mom says the TV won't be on at your house for a week. You:

A. Watch television at your friend's house. It's not on at your house.

B. Don't watch any television for a week.

C. Watch television before she gets home at night and turn it off when her car pulls up. It's an unfair punishment.

5 It's your first week in middle school. You're pretty sure that chewing gum is against the rules. You get caught with gum. You:

A. Tell the teacher you didn't know because no one told you.

B. Apologize for breaking the rules and face the consequences.

C. Pout and hope the teacher will feel sorry for you.

Best answers

1 **C** – A & B ARE BOTH DISHONEST because you didn't pay the correct amount to ride the rides.

2 **C** – A & B ARE BOTH DISHONEST because you didn't know the word at the time, and you might not have remembered it.

3 **A** – B & C AREN'T OUTRIGHT LIES but they're not honest either. You're being dishonest by what you are not saying.

(4) **B** – A IS NOT HONEST because you know she means no television anywhere, & C is outright disobedience.

(5) **B** – A ISN'T REALLY TRUE & C ISN'T PLAYING FAIR. It's not how God wants us to behave.

How did you do?

IF YOU GOT ALL FIVE OF THE BEST ANSWERS, good for you. You make right choices and try to be honest even if others wouldn't know the difference. You are honest in the little things as well as in bigger things.

IF YOU GOT 3-4 OF THE BEST ANSWERS, YOU ARE TRYING to make right choices, but you struggle with it. Ask God to give you an honest heart and help you make the best choice each time.

IF YOU GOT 1-2 OF THE BEST ANSWERS, you need to think about the choices you make. God sees you even when others don't, and He knows your heart. Ask God to change your heart and help you make the right choices from now on. He will answer that prayer.

AS A CHRISTIAN GIRL, IT ISN'T ENOUGH just not to lie or cheat. It's important to be honest in word and deed. Sometimes we lie just as much by what we don't say as what we do say. God's Spirit can help you make honest choices every time. Your integrity is worth more than you would gain by not being totally honest.

Sometimes we get trapped in our lies. They take on a life of their own. It takes another lie to cover up the first lie and then another lie to cover up that one. It can be hard to keep track of all the lies.

If you've developed the lying habit, try to break it. Ask God to help you be honest with yourself and others. He will. Stop and think before you speak. Ask yourself if what you're about to say is really true. Soon you will develop an honesty habit in place of the lying habit.

Can you think of a time when you didn't tell the truth? What happened?

_____

_____

_____

_____

Tune In!

The Lying Habit

There are several reasons for lying. You might lie . . .

✳ To keep from getting into trouble. Maybe you broke a dish you should pay for or didn't do your homework. If you can convince people you are innocent, you'll avoid the consequences.

✳ To impress others. You can make up stories about how popular you are, or how fast you swam at the last meet as long as no one can check to find out the truth.

✳ To get something. You might say you don't have any cookies so you can get more the next time. But lying is no way to get what you want.

✳ To get away with something. You might lie about which friend's house you are going to, or to your mom about watching television. You lie to get to do something you aren't usually allowed to do.

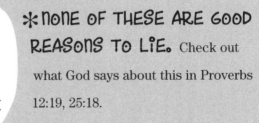

✳ NONE OF THESE ARE GOOD REASONS TO LIE. Check out what God says about this in Proverbs 12:19, 25:18.

Quiz #3

Are You a Good Test Taker?

Consider it pure joy, my brothers, whenever you face trials of many kinds, because you know that the testing of your faith develops perseverance.

~James 1:2-3

Bella watched as Mr. Miller walked down the aisle

handing out test. She started to feel sick.

"Are you okay?" her friend Meghan whispered.

"Just nervous about the test," Bella said. She tried to take deep breaths to calm herself.

"You knew all the answers when I quizzed you yesterday," Meghan said.

"I know," Bella answered. "But as soon as the test lands on my desk, I'll forget everything. I always do."

"Try reading through the whole test first. Some of the questions might give you the answers to other questions," Meghan said. "That's what I do. Answer what you know first, then tackle the rest."

Mr. Miller dropped the test on the desk in front of Bella. She took a deep breath and turned it over. She'd try what Meghan suggested. After all, it might even work!

We face all kinds of tests in life. There are math tests, spelling tests, achievement tests, and reading tests. Taking tests is a part of school. There are also tests in our Christian life. Sometimes God allows things to happen to see how we'll handle them. Sometimes school tests are easier than tests of our faith.

Some people have no trouble with tests, while others don't do so well. Anyone can improve her test-taking skills, though.

Quiz type: mental

Try the quiz below to see how your test-taking skills rate. Then read suggestions for taking tests and for facing tests in your Christian life.

 When it comes to study time I:

A. Have a certain time that I study every night.

B. Study when my mom says I have to study.

C. Don't study much.

 When the teacher announces a test I:

A. Don't worry about it until the night before the test.

B. Start studying early and study every day for a few minutes.

C. Don't worry about studying.

 During study time I usually:

A. E-mail my friends.

B. Spend half the time trying to find pencils and other supplies.

C. Get my stuff organized before I start studying.

If I don't understand what I'm studying I:

A. Ask a teacher, parent, or friend who can explain it to me.

B. Read it again and try to understand it.

C. Skip it.

 To prepare for a test I:

A. Cram as much as I can.

B. Forget all about it.

C. Have a parent or friend quiz me with review questions, and then do something fun or relaxing when we're done.

 The night before the test I:

A. Stay up late studying.

B. Stay up late watching TV.

C. Get at least 8 hours of sleep.

 The morning of the test I:

A. Skip breakfast because I'm too nervous.

B. Grab a yogurt for the road.

C. Eat a well-balanced breakfast.

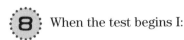
8 When the test begins I:

A. Start writing down answers.

B. Listen to the teacher's instructions then read them for myself.

C. Start thinking about what I want to do when I get home from school.

9 During the test if I don't know the answer to a question I:

A. Do the rest of the test, hope another question will give me a clue, and then make my best guess.

B. Leave it blank.

C. Make up an answer.

10 When I get my test back I:

A. Stuff it in my backpack.

B. Decide I'd better study more next time.

C. Look it over to see what I missed so I'll do better next time.

ANSWERS. Write the number of points you get for each question on the line. Then add them up.

1. A. 2 points   B. 1 point   C. 0 points ___1___

2. A. 1 point   B. 2 points   C. 0 points ___2___

3. A. 0 points   B. 1 point   C. 2 points ___2___

4. A. 2 points   B. 1 point   C. 0 points ___2___

5. A. 1 point   B. 0 points   C. 2 points ___2___

6. A. 1 point   B. 0 points   C. 2 points ___2___

7. A. 0 points   B. 1 point   C. 2 points ___2___

8. A. 1 point   B. 2 points   C. 0 points ___2___

9. A. 2 points   B. 0 points   C. 1 point ___2___

10. A. 0 points   B. 1 point   C. 2 points ___2___

TOTAL _____

How did you do? ☀

❀ **14-20 "FLYING HIGH"** You do well on tests because you value study time every night. You're organized and ready to hit the books after school. You start studying for tests early so you can study in short segments and not try to cram it all in the night before the test. Instead, you just need a quick review, then you can do something fun to help you relax and not worry about the test. On test day you are well rested and face the test confidently. Your excellent test-taking skills keep you on the honor roll every time!

7-13 "SHAKY GROUND"

You are making an effort when it comes to taking tests, but you need to start studying earlier. Ask a parent to quiz you over a small part of the material every night. You will remember things better if you learn them a little every day rather than trying to cram them in at the last minute. Your brain just doesn't absorb it all when you cram. Get at least 8-10 hours of sleep the night before a test. Start the day with a nutritious breakfast to fuel your body and brain. With a little extra work, you can bring your test scores up.

0-6 "SINKING FAST!"

You haven't developed the study skills that you need to do well in school. If you are struggling with the work ask a teacher to give you extra help. She might be able to assign you a tutor who can help you organize the material and come up with good study strategies. Have a friend or parent go over class material every night with you until you have learned it. Make sure you are listening in class too. Your teacher probably covers everything you need to know during class. Doing all of the homework assignments will help you prepare. It may take some hard work, but you can ace those tests!

Tune In!

Test Day Nerves?

If butterflies in your stomach keep you from doing your best on a test, try these ideas:

✳ Pray. Ask God to calm your mind and body.

✳ Study ahead of time so that you know the material well.

✳ Stop, relax, and breathe deeply.

✳ Give yourself a pep talk—"I know these answers, I can do it!"

✳ Memorize a special verse that you can quote to yourself, such as Philippians 4:13, "I can do everything through Him who gives me strength."

✳ If your mind goes blank, read through the test and maybe something on it will trigger the answers in your mind.

✳ If you find yourself doing poorly on tests because of nerves, talk to your parents and teacher about the problem. They may be able to figure out some way to help you.

SOME OF THE TESTS in our Christian life are temptations to do wrong. When this happens, fight back! Here's how:

AVOID IT. Stay away from situations that lead to sin. If you are tempted to shoplift, stay away from the store. If you are tempted to cheat on a test, ask to sit by yourself during the test. Do whatever you need to in order to avoid temptation.

FLEE IT. Run from tempting situations. Don't think that you can withstand them. God promises a way to escape from temptation (1 Corinthians 10:13). The way of escape may be leaving the tempting situation before you give in.

RESIST IT. When you can't flee the situation, just say "No!" This may mean taking a stand against popular classmates or even losing a friend. James 4:7-8 tells us that if we draw near to God, He will draw near to us; if we resist Satan, then Satan will flee from us.

CONFESS IT. God cares about you—and about the temptations you face daily! Confess them and ask for his help. When you fail, God has promised his forgiveness (1 John 1:9). Trying to hide your sin won't help; confessing it will make your heart clean.

Choose one of the test day nerve ideas above to try next time you have a test. Which one will you try?

_____

_____

After the test, write how it went.

_____

_____

_____

_____

  Next time your teacher announces a test, start studying 15 minutes a night until the test day and see if it makes a difference.

Quiz #4

How Much Do You Know About zzz's?

My help comes from the Lord,
the maker of heaven and earth.
He will not let your foot slip—
He who watches over you will not slumber.

~Psalm 121:2-3

Sometimes falling asleep at the wrong time can cause

real problems. It did for Eutychus. The Apostle Paul was preaching in the city of Troas. Since Paul and his fellow missionaries were leaving the next day, he spoke long into the night. Eutychus was sitting in a third-story

window listening, but it was midnight and he was getting sleepier and sleepier. He fell asleep and fell three stories to the ground. He was dead, but Paul brought him back to life. (You can read about it in Acts 20.) It's not a good idea to fall asleep in church if you are sitting in a window!

Fun Facts

On average, a koala bear sleeps up to 19 hours a day. And opossums, sloths, and armadillos spend about 80% of their lives sleeping!

Quiz type: physical

How much do you know about the world of zzz's? You probably know not to sit in an open window if you're sleepy! Test your sleep knowledge with this true or false quiz.

1.	The minimum amount of sleep you need is 8-10 hours.	TRUE	**FALSE**
2.	While you are sleeping your body is recharging for the next day	**TRUE**	FALSE
3.	Some people dream in black and white; others dream in color	**TRUE**	FALSE
4.	Going to bed at the same time each night helps you fall asleep.	**TRUE**	FALSE
5.	Drinking soda or hot chocolate before bed can keep you awake.	**TRUE**	FALSE
6.	Taking a warm bath before bed can help you fall asleep.	**TRUE**	FALSE
7.	You will sleep better in a dark room.	**TRUE**	FALSE
8.	Too much activity or exercise before bed can keep you awake.	TRUE	**FALSE**
9.	If you don't get enough sleep you might become overactive and teachers may think you are hyperactive.	**TRUE**	FALSE
10.	Not getting enough sleep can affect your schoolwork and your relationships with others in a bad way.	**TRUE**	FALSE

The answer to all ten questions is "True!" How many did you get right?

8-10 RIGHT: SWEET DREAMS! You understand what

it takes to get a good night's sleep. If you do those things, you will wake up well rested and ready to face the day.

6-8 RIGHT: NIGHTY-NIGHT! You are probably doing

some of the things that will help you get a good night's sleep. Reread the list and see if there are things you need to change.

5 OR FEWER RIGHT: TOSSING AND TURNING!

You might be in danger of falling asleep in math class! Read the reasons why each of the statements is true. Are there things you are doing that could keep you from getting a good night's sleep? Make a few changes and you may be surprised at how much better you feel in the morning!

FIND OUT WHY ALL THE ANSWERS ARE TRUE!

1. Your body needs a break from all your activity. Most kids 5-12 years old need 8 to 10 hours of sleep every night to recharge the mind and body.

2. Sleep is "down time" for your body, but that doesn't mean your body isn't doing anything. It is! While you're sleeping, your body's

$$2x-4=10$$
$$2x=10-4$$
$$2x=14$$

major organs keep right on working, and your body produces hormones. Some scientists say that when you sleep, your brain sorts through information from your day, replaces your body's chemicals, and may even solve problems!

3. This is true, but no one is sure why. Do you dream in black and white or color? If you're not sure, try to remember some of your dreams and think about what things looked like in those dreams.

4. Going to bed and waking up at about the same time every day— even on weekends—helps your body get into a routine.

5. Hot chocolate and many sodas have caffeine in them. Caffeine is a stimulant. It gets you wound up instead of settled down.

6. A warm bath can help your body relax, making it easier to get to sleep.

7. A dark room is one of the most helpful things for sleeping. The sun tells your body whether it's time to be awake or asleep. If too much light comes in your window at night, it can keep you awake even if you're tired. Ask your parents to help you install a curtain if you need it.

8. Exercise and activity stimulate your body. Read a book or listen to music before bed instead.

9. True! Sometimes not enough sleep makes you feel groggy and inattentive. Other times just the opposite happens, and you become too active and hyper.

10. When your body doesn't get enough rest, you aren't able to think clearly. You have a hard time following directions. Schoolwork that usually seems easy can be difficult. Not enough sleep affects your moods, too, and you can become cranky, even with your friends.

You might not feel like all of these items are true for you. And they may not be. These are the ideas that sleep experts find to be true for most people.

Try this Having a bedtime routine helps you fall asleep easier and feel more rested. Develop your own nighttime habits. You could include some of the suggestions below. Circle or highlight three of these to try, and do them at the same time every night. For instance, you might take a warm shower at 8 p.m., read your Bible at 8:15, and then listen to music from 8:30 until 9:00 while you fall asleep.

* Listen to relaxing music
* Read a book
* Read your Bible
* Pray
* Write in a journal
* Listen to an audio book
* Take a warm bath or shower

Make It

Need to get some sleep? Make this cute door hanger to let others know you're sleeping.

You Need: ⬅

* Discarded CD (don't use your brother's favorite music CD!)
* Craft foam in different colors depending on which CD animal you want to make.
* Scissors
* Glue
* Wiggle eyes
* Chenille stems
* Pompons
* Markers
* 18" of Ribbon

41

To Make a Door Hanger:

Look at the illustrations and choose which animal you want to make. You can even create your own.

1. Trace the CD onto the color craft foam you want for the animal you are making. For the ladybug, you need a circle of red, and a partial circle of black for the front of the bug; dark brown for the bear, green for the turtle, black or another color for the spider. You won't be able to read words on the black, so you may want to be creative with the spider color.

2. Glue both ends of the ribbon to the label side of the CD. It will form a loop in order for you to hang your door sign on your door handle.

3. If you are making a spider, glue four chenille stems to the CD, sticking out both sides at this time.

4. Glue the circle of craft foam over the ribbon. Allow it to dry.

5. Add the lighter colored pieces on the bear or turtle. Glue the black piece over the red for the ladybug.

6. Add wiggle eyes and pompon noses as desired.

7. Draw the middle line and spots on the ladybug. You could also make the spots from craft foam if desired.

8. Write words such as "Shhh sleeping," "Be beary quiet," (for the bear) or "Do not disturb," on your door hanger.

9. Hang it on your door while you sleep.

Quiz #5

Are You a Mary or a Martha?

Worship the Lord with gladness; come before Him with joyful songs.

~Psalm 100:2

Mary and Martha were two very different sisters.

One day Jesus visited them in their home. Martha busily went about her tasks since there was a lot to do when visitors came by. Maybe she was cleaning or perhaps she was preparing a special meal for Jesus. Mary, on

the other hand, sat at Jesus' feet and listened to what He had to say to her. This made Martha frustrated! She was busy working, and Mary was just sitting around!

Martha complained to Jesus: "Lord, don't you care that my sister has left me to do the work by myself? Tell her to help me!"

"Martha, Martha," the Lord answered, "you are worried and upset about many things, but only one thing is needed. Mary has chosen what is better, and it will not be taken away from her."

What did Mary chose that was better? She recognized who Jesus really was, and she spent time with Him.

Quiz type: spiritual

Who are you more like—Mary or Martha? Take the quiz to find out.

Read the sentences in the lists below. Put a check mark by each sentence that is true about you.

LIST **a**

___ I have a special time when I read my Bible each day.

___ I have a list of things I pray for each day.

✓ While I read my Bible and pray, I'm listening to hear if God speaks to my heart.

✓ I listen to the Bible reading at church.

___ I listen (really listen!) to the sermon at church.

___ I wholeheartedly take part in the singing at church.

✓ When I pray, I praise God for who He is and for the things He's done for me.

LIST **B**

✓ I offer to pass out the Sunday school papers and supplies.

___ I volunteer to clean up the room after Sunday school.

___ Whenever I hear about someone who needs help, I do what I can to help.

___ I am involved in the projects my church group does.

___ I rake leaves or shovel snow for older people who can't do it themselves.

___ When we have visitors at our house, I help my mom get things ready.

___ If someone asks me to help with a job, I do it cheerfully.

Count how many checks you have ☼

COUNT how many checks you have in list A and write the number here: ___3___

COUNT how many checks you have in list B and write the number here: ___6___

❀ IF YOU HAVE FOUR OR MORE CHECKS IN THE FIRST LIST, you are like Mary. You know that it's important to spend time with Jesus through Bible reading, prayer, church, and praise. That doesn't mean it's not important to serve the Lord, only that worship is the more important of the two.

♡ ♡ ♡

☼ **IF YOU HAVE FOUR OR MORE CHECKS IN THE SECOND LIST,** you are like Martha. You are busy showing your love for Jesus by serving. Jesus didn't tell Martha that it was wrong to be busy doing things. He just wanted her to realize that it was more important to take time out to spend with Him. How else can we serve people if we don't take time to receive from God first?

🐱 **IF YOU HAVE FOUR OR MORE CHECKS IN BOTH LISTS,** that's great! You make time to be with Jesus, and you show your love for Him by serving Him at church and home. Both are important, and it's terrific that you are already busy worshipping and serving.

❀ **IF YOU DON'T HAVE FOUR CHECKS IN EITHER LIST,** stop and think of some ways you can be more involved in worship and service. Maybe you can get up 15 minutes earlier in the morning to read your Bible and pray. Ask your Sunday school teacher or a parent about ways you could be more involved in helping others for Jesus. Ask God to show you ways to be both a worshiper and a server.

GOD Connection

IT'S IMPORTANT TO BOTH WORSHIP AND SERVE. You worship through Bible reading, prayer and singing praises to God. You serve when you help your mom by cooking dinner or babysitting your sibling so she can have a break. There are many more ways to worship and serve. Ask God to help you find ways to do both this week.

Try this Set aside 15 minutes a day this week to worship God. Try these ideas:

✳ Sing songs to God.

✳ Read some of the Psalms aloud.

✳ Pray some of the Psalms as your own prayers to God.

✳ Tell God three things you like most about Him.

✳ Thank God for ten things.

✳ Be still and listen for God to speak to you.

Going to church is an important part of worshiping God. You can make the bag below to carry your Bible and a notebook and pen to church.

You Need:

* A denim bag in your favorite color
* Fun-shaped buttons (from a craft store) in coordinating colors
* Ribbon in a coordinating color
* Fabric glue
* Markers

To Make a Bible Holder:

1. Tie the ribbon into small bows.
2. Arrange the bows and buttons on the front of the bag (see the illustrations for ideas).
3. Secure by using fabric glue.
4. Decorate your bag with fabric paints. Allow it to dry.
5. Use it to carry your Bible and supplies to church.

Quiz #6

How Are Your Manners?

Let the peace of Christ rule in your hearts, since as members of one body you were called to peace. And be thankful.

~Colossians 3:15

Good manners are ways of showing respect and

courtesy to others. When you are courteous you put others first and think of their needs and feelings.

Are there times when you don't know what to do, how to act, or what to say? Of course there are. Jenna, a girl your age, had the same problem. She received an invitation to a friend's birthday party. When she arrived at the party in jeans and a T-shirt with a brightly wrapped present, she quickly realized something was wrong. All the other kids were dressed up. This wasn't your typical party, it was a formal dinner. Nothing Jenna had done before prepared her for this. There was lots of extra silverware and small plates meant to be used for different dishes. Jenna watched the others, hoping to copy them, and was relieved to see that most of them, while dressed up, had no idea what to do with all the silverware either.

You aren't likely to find yourself in that situation, but there may be times when you're not sure of the correct thing to do. Will you be ready?

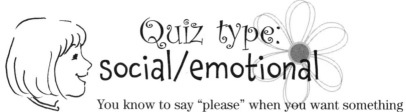

Quiz type: social/emotional

You know to say "please" when you want something and "thank you" when you get it. You know to say, "Excuse me" when you bump someone or need to interrupt. But sometimes it's not easy to know what to do. Read each situation below and decide which of the answers sounds most like what you'd do.

 1 You're in the mall with your dad. You see your teacher a few stores down. Your dad hasn't met your teacher yet. What do you do?

A. Call to her, "Miss Smith, I want you to meet my dad."

B. Walk up to her and say, "Miss Smith I'd like you to meet my dad, Mr. _____."

C. Wait for her to come introduce herself to your dad.

2 You are at a family reunion and your mother introduces you to a great-aunt you've never met. She looks really old and you aren't sure what to say. What do you do?

A. Say, "If you're my great-aunt you must be really old."

B. Wait for her to say something to you.

C. Shake hands and say, "It's nice to meet you."

3. The phone rings. Your dad's boss wants to talk to him, but your dad is in the shower. What do you say to your dad's boss?

A. "My dad's in the shower. Bye."

B. "My dad can't come to the phone right now, may I take a message or have him call you back?"

C. "What do you want?"

4. You are at the mall with your sister. She buys a cookie and eats it all. Later you buy a bag of candy. You know she really likes it, but she already had a cookie. What should you do?

A. Eat it in front of her. She ate her cookie in front of you.

B. Save it for later when she's not around.

C. Offer her a piece.

5 You're at a friend's house and her parents serve you something for dinner you don't recognize. There's a bowl of some sort of sauce too. You don't know whether to cut the mystery food and dip it in the sauce or pour the sauce on top. What do you do?

A. Say, "What in the world is this?"

B. Ask to be excused to the bathroom.

C. Start eating the rest of your food and watch to see what everyone else does with the mystery food.

6 Your grandmother visits your family for Christmas. She gives you a sweater. It has a kitten on the front. You know your friends will die laughing if they see you wear it. You can see that your grandmother is waiting for you to say something. You don't want to lie and say you love it, but you don't want to hurt her feelings either. What do you do?

A. Say, "I don't really wear sweaters."

B. Ask, "Can I exchange this for a skateboard?"

C. Say, "It was really nice of you to think of me, Grandma."

7 You are at a really nice restaurant when your fork takes on a life of its own and flies out of your hand with a piece of meat attached. What do you do?

A. Tell your waitress what happened and ask for a new fork.

B. Go get it and wipe it off with your napkin.

C. Pretend it didn't happen and eat the rest of your food with your spoon.

8 Just as you take a big bite of food at a party, an adult asks you what grade you're in at school. What do you do?

A. Finish chewing, swallow, and answer.

B. Hold up six fingers for sixth grade.

C. Put your hand over your mouth so she doesn't see the food when you answer.

9 You are eating in public when suddenly you let out a huge burp! Everyone looks toward your table. You:

A. Duck under the table.

B. Point at your little brother.

C. Say "excuse me" and keep eating.

You are at a birthday party for a girl in your class at school. You don't really know her well. The party isn't much fun because she's bossing everyone around so much. You:

A. Tell her if she doesn't stop it you'll go home.

B. Try to be patient with her. She's probably just excited about the party and wants everything to go her way.

C. Tell her mom to make her stop being so bossy.

ANSWERS:

1. B. You don't want to call to her because it's not polite to use a loud voice public places, and it might sound pretty rude to call out to your teacher. Introducing her is a good thing to do. If you look in a manners book it will tell you to introduce the older person first when you're introducing two or more people to each other. But really, if you are polite about it, it probably doesn't matter most of the time.

2. C. There are some things that it's just not polite to comment on, such as a person's age, weight, how much money they have, and other topics that aren't your business. But it is always okay to shake hands and say something like, "Pleased to meet you" or "Hello ma'am."

3. B. Don't volunteer information about why someone can't come to the phone. Ask if you may take a message or if the caller would like the person to call them back when they can.

4. B OR C. It's impolite to eat in front of someone who doesn't have something to eat herself—even though she did it to you. Either wait until she's not around or share. You don't have to split the bag with her—it's yours. Just offer her a couple of pieces.

5. C. Start eating the foods you are familiar with and watch to see what people do with the mystery food. Don't be afraid to try something new even if you're not sure you'll like it. If you try a couple of bites and don't like it, just eat your other food.

6. C. You haven't said you loved the sweater, but at the same time you've let her know you appreciate her thinking of you. And it wouldn't hurt to go and put the sweater on while you open the rest of your gifts. No one but your family will see you in it, and it'll make her day.

7. A. Embarrassing things happen all the time. Just handle it calmly. Politely ask a waiter or waitress for another utensil. You aren't the first one who's dropped a piece of silverware in a restaurant.

8. A. Chew and swallow before answering. She'll realize what you're doing and will wait for your answer.

9. C. This happens to all of us. You may as well 'fess up, excuse yourself, and keep eating. If you don't make a big deal about it, no one else will either.

10. B. Leaving would look rude even though you really aren't having much fun. Try to be patient and understand that she just wants things to go her way at her party. Maybe you can tactfully make some suggestions. But if not, just hang out, and thank her for inviting you as you leave. Try to say something nice like, "That was a nice cake you had," but don't say you had a good time if you didn't.

If you got most of them right, good for you! Your manners are in place both at home and when you're out. Using good manners is polite and shows others that you respect their feelings.

DOES GOD CARE ABOUT good manners? Of course He does. Using manners shows respect to those around us, and God is all about treating others right. Philippians 2 tells us that we should think of others' needs ahead of our own. Using good manners is one way to do that.

 Could your table manners use a boost? Circle the pictures that are good manners and put an X over those that are bad manners.

Quiz #7

What Kind of Smart Are You?

There are different kinds of gifts, but the same Spirit. There are different kinds of service, but the same Lord.

~1 Corinthians 12:4-5

When you think of "smart," you might think about how well you did on your last math test or the grade you got on your history report. If you get straight A's on your report card, people probably tell you that you're smart. But there are many ways to be smart. In the 1980's, Howard Gardner wrote a famous book describing eight different kinds of smart. Try the quiz below to find out what kind of smart you are.

Once you find out what kind of smart you are, you can discover some ways to use your smarts for God.

Quiz type: mental

Read the sentences in each list. Check all of the ones that describe you.

List

_____ I like to play word games like Scrabble or Catch Phrase more than other games.

_____ I read one or more books a week just for fun.

_____ I keep a journal or diary.

_____ I can tell stories and jokes well.

_____ I enjoy writing letters to others.

_____ I do well when I have to write a school report.

_____ I can express myself well when I speak and when I write.

_____ English and reading are my best subjects.

LIST B

___ I enjoy games that use sight such as Pictionary more than other games.

___ I notice how things look more than my friends do.

___ I see patterns in the sky or sand.

___ I can navigate for my parents on trips using a map.

___ I like to make videos of family activities.

___ I am good at mazes and jigsaw puzzles.

___ I use diagrams and drawings to help me study.

___ Art is my best subject.

LIST C

___ I like to play music games like karaoke or Name That Tune more than other games.

___ I can listen to a new song and then hear it in my head.

___ I enjoy playing one or more instruments.

___ I learn things better when I put them to a rhythm or tune.

___ I am often told that I have "an ear for music."

___ I can clap out a rhythm easily.

___ I remember commercial jingles and can sing them.

___ Music and band are my best subjects.

LIST D

___ I enjoy movement games such as Twister or Charades more than other games.

___ I am often told I have good coordination (hands and feet working well together during sports or exercise).

___ I am good at video games that require quick hand movements.

___ I enjoy taking part in one or more sports activities.

___ I think most clearly when I'm running or active.

___ I learn best when I can touch and handle objects or do experiments.

___ I prefer running, biking, and playing sports to talking on the phone or reading.

___ My best subjects are PE and classes where I make projects with my hands.

LIST e

___ My favorite games are those that require planning, such as chess or Monopoly.

___ I can easily solve brain teasers and riddles.

___ I can solve math problems in my head.

What Kind of Smart Are You?

__ I am bothered when someone comes up with an answer that doesn't make sense.

__ I solve problems by thinking them through step-by-step, not by "gut feeling" (when you just feel that something is right).

__ I often put things into categories (group my books by type or by author, hang my clothes by color and so on).

__ I enjoy the computer lab at school.

__ Math and science are my best subjects.

LIST

___ I like games that involve people, such as Family Feud, more than other games.

___ I can tell what people are feeling by watching them.

___ I notice people as I walk by them in the mall.

___ I give my friends "pep talks" (cheer them up) when they are discouraged.

___ I like helping my friends find solutions to their problems.

___ I like working on group projects.

___ I enjoy going to parties and social events.

___ My best classes include working in groups.

LIST G

____ I like games I can play alone more than group games.

____ I usually know why I'm in the mood I'm in.

____ I keep a journal and often write about what I'm feeling.

____ I know what I'm good at and what I'm not good at.

____ I set goals and achieve them.

____ I like hobbies and activities I can do by myself.

____ I would rather work alone than with a group.

____ Classes in which I can do individual projects are my best classes.

LIST H

____ I like games I can play outside.

____ I enjoy nature walks where I can learn and identify plants and trees.

____ I look up the birds, trees, or flowers I see to find out what kind they are.

____ I do activities to help the environment (recycle, plant trees, etc.).

____ I sometimes can tell what the weather is going to be just by being outside.

____ I like to be outdoors more than indoors.

_✓_ I notice sights, sounds, smells, and flavors more than my
friends do.

___ Science is my best subject.

How did you do?

COUNT HOW MANY CHECKS you have in each list. You may have
checks in many of the categories. That's good because it means you have
strengths in many areas. Circles with four or more checks are your strong
areas. Read below to find out what kind of smart each circle represents.

A e G

LIST A: WORD SMART

You speak and read well. Words interest you. You might enjoy making
up rhymes and tongue twisters. When it comes to Scrabble, you are more
skilled than your friends. You have an advantage at school because much
of your school day consists of reading, listening, and speaking—and that's
how you learn best.

If you want to try something new, learn a foreign language—you
can check out CDs or DVDs at your public library—or write poetry, or a
speech or article to convince others of something you believe in strongly.
Listen to an audiobook while you follow along in the printed book.

☼ LIST B: PICTURE SMART

You see designs, colors, and patterns better than most people do. You use these skills when you use a map to navigate while your mom or dad drives, or when you rearrange your room to get a certain look. You are good at jigsaw puzzles and mazes. You learn best by drawing or using charts and graphs.

If you want to try something new, offer to decorate a classroom bulletin board or design posters to illustrate the class rules. Perhaps you can design and paint the backgrounds for your school play. Ask if you can turn in a series of illustrations instead of your next written book report. Make a model of a famous building or landmark out of Legos.

🐱 LIST C: MUSIC SMART

You might find yourself tapping your foot to the music that's in your head. You are probably in band or chorus if your school has them. If not, you still sing along with your favorite music at home. You memorize things like state capitals or the names of Presidents by putting them to music, because that's how you learn best.

If you want to try something new, listen to a totally different kind of music than you normally do. You can check out CDs from your public library. Write a jingle advertising your favorite soft drink. Learn a new Bible verse by singing it to a familiar tune such as "Mary had a Little Lamb," or "Row, Row, Row Your Boat."

LIST D: BODY SMART

You have natural athletic ability. People notice how coordinated you are, and no one tells you that you have two left feet. You are also good at things other than sports that require coordination, such as pottery or acting in a play. Try memorizing your times tables or spelling words while skipping rope, bouncing a basketball, or acting them out, because you learn best using your body.

If you want to try something new, choose a craft that requires coordination such as pottery, woodworking, or sewing. Learn a new dance or create your own gymnastics routine.

LIST E: NUMBER/LOGIC SMART

You do well not only in math but also in science and in other areas that require logical thinking. You have an advantage at school because you ace math and science. You learn best by putting things in categories and solving problems. On vacation you might prefer to visit a planetarium or science museum rather than the beach. Games like chess, checkers, Clue, and Stratego are easy for you.

If you want to try something new, try writing some brain teasers or riddles for your friends to solve. Go grocery shopping with your mom and use a calculator to figure out which brand has the best price by figuring the cost per ounce.

LIST F: PEOPLE SMART

You can tell when your mom has been pushed past her limits or when your friend is ready to burst into tears. Not only that, but you enjoy listening to their problems and helping solve them. You are good at getting people to do things, but be careful not to talk them into doing only what you want. You enjoy parties where you can talk to old friends but also meet new people. You aren't afraid to approach people and start a conversation. You learn best by working with other people.

If you want to try something new, try volunteering at a nursing home where you can use your people skills to make others happy. Tutor a struggling student or be a buddy to a new student.

LIST G: SELF SMART

You spend time thinking about who you are, what you like, what you are good at, and what you want to accomplish. You understand why you do the things you do, and why you feel the things you feel. Sometimes you write down your feelings. Time alone doesn't bother you because you use it to think and reflect. You learn best by yourself.

If you want to try something new, record your thoughts and feelings in a journal each night. Write a poem that shows your feelings about something. Choose a place to be your special "alone spot."

☀ LIST 4: NATURE SMART

You enjoy nature walks and remember the names of plants and trees. You are curious about the outdoors. Environmental issues interest you. You may find that your senses of sight, hearing, smell, taste, and touch are stronger than those of your friends. You see patterns in your surroundings that other people don't notice. You probably have one or more collections from nature—leaves, insects, shells, or other objects.

If you want to try something new, plant a garden or create a terrarium using a glass jar or aquarium. Make a model of the solar system and ask your teacher if you can display it in the classroom.

 **NO MATTER WHAT KIND** of "smart" you are, always remember to be God-smart. God cares about everything you do. Listen to Him, talk to Him, and include Him in your every day life. All your talents and abilities are from God, and He wants you to use them for Him.

Think about a way that you can use your unique abilities for God this week. Here are some ideas:

WORD SMART—Use your words to write stories or poems about Jesus.

PICTURE SMART—Try designing a pamphlet to share the gospel or create a bulletin board for the children's Sunday school class.

MUSIC SMART—Praise God through music by listening to (or singing) praise songs or playing them on an instrument.

BODY SMART—If you play on a sports team, other students probably look to you as a role model. You can be a good witness for Jesus by the way you act.

NUMBER/LOGIC SMART—You can use your reasoning ability to persuade others about the truth of God's love and His plan for us.

PEOPLE SMART—You can use your compassionate nature to reach out to others and share Jesus with them.

SELF SMART—You might want to keep a journal about daily events, or a diary about your Christian faith.

NATURE SMART—Use your knowledge about nature to teach others about how God's world works.

Quiz #8

Are You a Healthy Eater?

Do you not know that your body is a temple of the Holy Spirit, who is in you, whom you have received from God? You are not your own; you were bought at a price. Therefore honor God with your body.

~1 Corinthians 6:19-20

Heather took her place on the starting line for the
100-meter dash. She was trying out for the middle school
track team along with fifteen other girls. Heather
hoped she'd make it. She'd already done long
jump and shot put, but now she was feeling
worn out, and she still had the 400-meter
dash, high jump, and javelin to do. Heather
felt more like taking a nap than throwing a
javelin or trying to get over a bar.

Heather wished she'd had more than
a diet soda and bag of chips for lunch. Maybe if she'd eaten
healthier, she'd have more energy for the try-outs. Heather vowed to
change her eating habits if she made the team.

Quiz type: physical

God gave us wonderful bodies made in His image. It's our job to take
the best care of them that we can. One way to do that is by maintaining
healthy eating habits. Take the quiz below to see if you are a healthy eater.

1 It's snack time. What do you have?

A. Doesn't matter as long as it's chocolate!

B. Just a diet soda, thanks.

C. Yogurt or a piece of fruit.

D. A can of soda and chips.

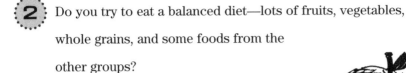

2 Do you try to eat a balanced diet—lots of fruits, vegetables, whole grains, and some foods from the other groups?

A. I eat mostly from the dessert group.

B. I try to eat a variety of fruits and vegetables along with whole grains and foods from the other groups.

C. I eat exactly the amounts recommended and avoid all sweets.

D. I eat a little more sweets and fewer vegetables than recommended.

3 Do you eat treats such as cookies and cakes?

A. Never!

B. I get a treat in my lunch sometimes.

C. I live for chocolate.

D. One sweet treat a day.

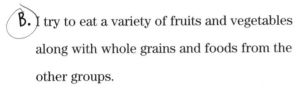

4 How much water do you drink a day?

A. How much water is in soda?

B. Probably a gallon.

C. 1–2 cups

D. 4–8 cups

5. Do you ever try new vegetables?

A. When my mom puts them on my plate.

B. Vegetables? No way!

C. Sure, I'll try anything once.

D. I only eat vegetables.

6. If I go to a fast food restaurant I always get:

A. Salad and water.

B. Something from the healthy choice menu.

C. A kid's meal or combo.

D. A double burger with cheese and loads of fries.

7. If I don't have time to sit down and eat breakfast I grab:

A. A jelly doughnut and soda.

B. Water and a rice cake.

C. Toaster pastry and carton of juice.

D. Yogurt and carton of juice.

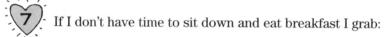

How did you do? Add up your points.

1. A=2   B=4   C=3   D=1   _3_ points

2. A=1   B=3   C=4   D=2   _3_ points

Are You a Healthy Eater?

3. A=4　B=3　C=1　D=2　*2* _____ points

4. A=1　B=4　C=2　D=3　*3* _____ points

5. A=2　B=1　C=3　D=4　*2* _____ points

6. A=4　B=3　C=2　D=1　*2* _____ points

7. A=1　B=4　C=2　D=3　*4* _____ points

14 _____ Total points

🌼 7-12 UNBALANCED DIET. There is more to food than

fries and chocolate. Try replacing the snacks that lack nutritional value
with others that have what your body needs. Replace chips with yogurt or
a piece of fruit. A strong and healthy body needs good fuel.

☀ 13-18 SLIGHTLY OFF-BALANCE.

Some of your choices lack nutritional value.
Occasional treats are okay, but also
choose snacks such as raisins or
apples. The important thing is that your
body is getting the nutrition it needs to grow and
function well.

🐱 19-24 WELL-BALANCED. You do

a good job of balancing healthy food with treats.
Continue to make wise choices but allow yourself
some fun food too.

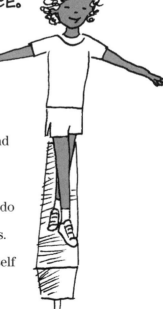

✿ **25-28 OVERBOARD.** Whoa. Are you for real? You need more than salad and water to maintain a healthy body. Treats are okay, too, as long as you only have them occasionally. Some people go overboard on sweets and junk food, but it's possible to go overboard on trying to eat too healthy or too little. If you feel you need to lose weight, talk your parents who can take you to a doctor. There are many healthy ways to do it.

GOD CREATED YOU in an amazing and wonderful way (Psalm 139:14). You honor God by taking the best care possible of your amazing body. One way to do that is to make nutritious choices when you eat. That doesn't mean you can't have any sweets, but make sure that most of the time you give your body the fuel it needs so that you'll be the healthiest you that you can be.

Try this Write down what you eat every day for a week. Are you eating from all of the food groups with most of your food coming from the fruits and vegetable group? What changes do you need to make?

Make It

It's important to eat healthy snacks. Here's cute snack sack you can make for lunch or snacks on the go.

You Need: ↙

* 12" cut from the leg of an old pair of jeans; cut off the hem if you use the bottom of the leg
* lace—long enough to go around the width of the jeans
* fabric glue
* 18-24" of inseam from a pair of old jeans (cut thin like a strap)
* fabric or puffy paint

To Make a Snack Sack: ↙

1. Turn piece of jean leg inside out.

2. Glue the bottom closed. Let dry.

3. Turn the jean leg right side out.

4. Line up the top of the lace with the top of the bag.

5. Glue the lace to the material.

6. Glue one end of the handle inside the bag in front of the side seam about one inch down.

7. Glue the other end of the handle behind the other side seam about one inch down.

8. Decorate or personalize the front of your bag with fabric or puffy paint.

Quiz #9

Are You a Follower or a Leader?

Follow my example, as I follow the example of Christ.

~1 Corinthians 11:1

It was time for class elections, and the seventh grade art class was making posters to support their favorite candidate for class president.

"Why don't you run for president, Kaylee?" Amber asked. "Everyone likes you. You'd be sure to win."

"I don't think I'd make a good president," Kaylee said. "I like to have fun and do things, but I don't like to be in charge. I'm not a good leader."

"Why not?" Amber asked. "I bet you could make a lot of good changes around here."

"I don't like to be in front. A leader has to be able to speak to a whole group and convince them to do things. I can't do that. I'm more of a behind the scenes worker. I think I'd rather join one of the committees and help out where I'm needed rather than be in a leadership position."

"I guess you're right," Amber said. "I wouldn't be a good leader either. I guess I'll vote for Nicholas for president. He already helps lead the church youth group. He'd be a good class president."

"I'll vote for him, too," Kaylee said.

Quiz type: social/emotional

Some people are born leaders while others are born followers. It takes both kinds of people to make a strong team. Take the quiz below to find out your style!

1 Your history teacher announces that you must build a teepee. You can do it alone or with a group. You:

A. Grab two friends and ask them to meet at your house after school to look up teepees on the Internet and make your plans.

B. Know it'll be easier to do it by yourself than try to get together with a group.

C. Look around for a fun group and join them.

2 Your school is having a carnival. You:

A. Volunteer to design a flyer about it on your home computer.

B. Volunteer to organize the booths.

C. Volunteer to help where needed.

3 Your church girls' group is having a campout. You:

A. Lead the devotions.

B. Help set up tents.

C. Wash dishes.

 4 If you were going to the beach would you rather:

A. Lie in the sun and read a book.

B. Throw a Frisbee with your friend.

C. Organize beach games for everyone to play.

 5 You are going to sign up for an after-school club. Which do you pick?

A. Yearbook

B. Cooking

C. Speech

Write your points for each question. Then add up all your points

1. A. 3 points   B. 1 point   C. 2 points   _____ points

2. A. 1 point   B. 3 points   C. 2 points   _____ points

3. A. 3 points   B. 2 points   C. 1 point   _2_ points

4. A. 1 point   B. 2 points   C. 3 points   _2_ points

5. A. 2 points   B. 1 point   C. 3 points   _____ points

                                   Total points   _____ points

❀ **12-15 PoINTS** You're a natural born leader! You like to be in charge and organize things. Talking in front of a group doesn't make you nervous, and people listen to what you have to say. Be careful not to be pushy though or people won't want to follow. You don't have to be in charge of every activity. It's important for others take the lead sometimes so make sure you know how to follow someone else who is a good leader, too. A good leader must know how to be a good servant first. Think of some of the great Bible leaders—Moses, Joshua, Jesus, Paul, and others. How are you like them? How can you use your leadership abilities for God?

☼ **8-11 PoINTS** You're a follower. And that's okay. Just make sure you're following the right people! Don't be swayed by peer pressure to do wrong. Remember, Jesus' disciples were followers. Make sure you are following Jesus, too. Followers who have a spirit of cooperation and willingness can be a great help to their leaders.

0-7 POINTS You'd rather work alone. You feel more comfortable doing the job yourself. That's okay sometimes, but try to get involved in some group activities, too. Some projects are more fun when you do them with a group. Being alone is good, but being alone all the time isn't. God created us to live our lives with one another. Find at least one friend and share fun times with them.

The Apostle Paul knew the key to being a leader. Jesus was his role model and Paul did exactly what he thought the Lord would do. That made him a strong, Christ-like leader. But not everyone is a leader. Some people are followers and behind-the-scenes workers. They are very necessary, too. Whether you're a leader or a support person, the important thing is to do what God calls you to do.

Look around you. Who is the leader in your class? Make a list of traits he or she demonstrates. Do these traits make him or her a good influence on others or not? What are the character traits of a good leader?

_____

_____

_____

_____

_____

Quiz #10

How Much Do You Know About the Bible?

Like newborn babies, crave pure spiritual milk, so that by it you may grow up in your salvation.

~1 Peter 2:2

You might have heard Bible stories read to you at home.

You probably heard the same stories at church. But how much do you really remember about those stories?

Quiz type: spiritual

Take the quiz below to see how much you know about people in the Bible.

 God promised this man that he would be blessed. God gave him a son even though he and his wife were old.

A. Noah   B. Moses   C. Abraham

 This man was told to build a big boat to save his family from the flood.

A. Noah   B. Moses

C. Abraham

 This young man was sold by his brothers.

A. David   B. Jacob   C. Joseph

 He was chosen to lead the people out of slavery.

A. Joseph   B. Noah   C. Moses

5 These were the two spies who believed God would help the people conquer the Promised Land.

A. Jacob and Esau B. Cain and Abel C. Joshua and Caleb

6 What woman picked up left over grain in Boaz's field and later married him?

A. Sarah   B. Ruth   C. Deborah

7 Who was told to dunk in the river to cure himself of leprosy?

A. Naaman   B. Elisha   C. Elijah

8 Who was taken up to heaven in a whirlwind?

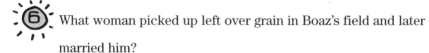

A. Elijah   B. Elisha

C. Samuel

9 What young man was taken to Babylon as a captive and prayed faithfully to God?

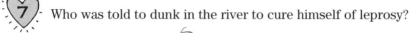

A. David   B. Daniel   C. Ezra

10 This prophet did not want to go to Nineveh and tried to run away from God.

A. Nahum   B. Joel   C. Jonah

11 Before he followed Jesus, Matthew was a:

A. doctor   B. tax collector   C. lawyer

12 He wanted to walk on water like Jesus.

A. Peter   B. John   C. James

13 Two women with this name saw the empty tomb.

A. Ruth   B. Lydia   C. Mary

14 Who was stoned to death for his beliefs?

A. John   B. Stephen   C. Luke

15 When Paul and Silas were thrown in jail they:

A. complained   B. prayed and sang   C. escaped

Check your answers!

HOLD THIS PAGE UP TO A MIRROR TO SEE HOW MANY YOU GOT CORRECT:

11. B	6. B	1. C
12. A	7. A	2. A
13. C	8. A	3. C
14. B	9. B	4. C
15. B	10. C	5. C

How many did you get right?

 **11–15 BiBLE SCHOLAR!** You have good Bible knowledge. Keep reading your Bible so you can learn even more.

6–10 BiBLE LEARNER. You have a good start on learning your Bible people and stories. Listen closely in Sunday school and church. Be sure to take time to read your Bible at home so you can learn even more.

1–5 DON'T GiVE UP! Study your Bible stories and try again!

CACC CBC
BAC

Rolemodel Puzzle

Why do you think God put stories about these particular people in the Bible? Decode the verse below for a hint.

Look at the balloons. Find the balloon with a "1" in it. Unscramble the word and write it on line one. Do this until you can read the verse.

_____ with _____ in _____ _____

1   2   3   4

_____, _____, and _____ _____ of

5   6   7   8

_____ who _____ _____ to the _____

9   10   11   12

we _____ _____ .

13   14

~Philippians 3:17

Puzzle answer at the end of the book.

God gives us both good and bad examples to learn from in the Bible. Who is one Bible character whose example you can follow?

_____

_____

_____

THE BIBLE CHARACTERS

mentioned in this quiz had no idea that we would be reading their stories thousands of years later and still be learning from them. In the same way, we don't know who is watching us each day and learning from us. What would someone observing you today say about your life?

Here are some favorite Bible stories. Why not read one a day or even one a week? Even if you've read these stories before, you might find something new in them that you missed last time.

Creation .... Genesis 1

Noah's Ark... Genesis 6-9

God Tests Abraham .... Genesis 22

Baby Moses.. Exodus 2

The Walls of Jericho............................. Joshua 6

David and Goliath.................................. 1 Samuel 17

Elijah and the Prophets of Baal.......... 1 Kings 18

The Fiery Furnace................................. Daniel 3

Jesus is Born.. Luke 2

Jesus Calms the Storm........................ Luke 8

Jesus Feeds the Crowd........................ Luke 9

The Empty Tomb.................................... John 20

Jesus Talks to Saul .... Acts 9

Do you have a favorite Bible story? Share it with your best friend and talk about why it's so great!

Quiz #11

What's Your Learning Style?

Do your best to present yourself to God as one approved, a workman who does not need to be ashamed and who correctly handles the word of truth.

~2 Timothy 2:15

The verse on the previous page says that we should know how to use God's Word. To do that we need to learn God's Word first. Not everyone learns things the same way. Knowing how you learn can help you study better, understand more and remember things longer, whether you are learning God's Word or math facts.

Kelsey knows she learns best by listening when things are explained to her. So she does well when her teacher explains subjects to the class, but not as well when she has to learn by reading from the textbook. At home she learns by making up rhymes to help her learn vocabulary words or definitions. If she has to read a book for a book report, she tries to get the book on CD at the library as well as the printed book. She follows along in the book as she hears it read. Knowing that she learns best by hearing things has helped Kelsey do better on homework and tests.

Quiz type: mental

Take the quiz below to find out how you learn best. Choose the picture in front of the answer that sounds most like what you would do. Try to choose an answer for each question even if you've never been in that situation.

1 You've moved to a new school. You aren't really sure where everything is located. The best way for you to find things would be to have:

 A map that shows you where everything is.

 Someone to explain to you where to find what you need.

 A guide to walk you where you need to go.

2 You are going to take a test about the states. You have to be able to label them on a blank map. The best way for you to learn them would be:

 Studying a map with the states labeled on it, and then trying to write the state names on a blank map.

 Singing or saying the states' names out loud while pointing to them on a map.

 Cutting the practice map your teacher gave you into pieces and trying to put it back together like a puzzle.

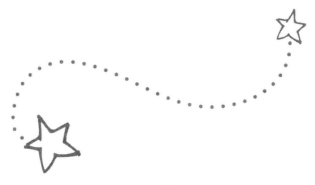

3 It's time to work with fractions: dividing shapes into halves, thirds, and fourths. You will learn this best by:

Study the drawings in your book.

Have the teacher or a friend explain to you how to do it.

Practice cutting pizzas into those fractions.

4 You need to learn a verse for your Sunday school class. The best way to learn it would be:

Write it on your dry-erase board where you can see it. Erase a word at a time and try to see the missing word in your mind. Do this until you know the whole verse.

Say the verse to a rhythm until you can say it without looking.

Bounce a basketball. Say one word for each bounce. Do this until you can "bounce out" the whole verse.

5 Your teacher gives the first word of a spelling test. You know how to spell the word because:

You can see the word in your mind.

You can hear yourself spelling the word.

You know how it feels to write the word.

6 You have a book report due. You haven't read the book yet. You prefer to:

 Read the book.

 Listen to the audio book.

 See the movie with friends.

 7 You need to get the book report ready. You plan to:

 Do a written report.

 Do an oral report.

 Act out a scene.

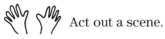 **8** You need to do a science project about how crystals form. You think the best way is to:

 Write a report and include charts and graphs to illustrate the process.

 Do a recorded presentation on how crystals form.

   Grow crystals at home and take them in to science class.

9 You need to know how many cups are in a pint, how many pints in a quart and how many quarts in a gallon. The best way to remember is:

 Draw a picture showing the amounts.

 Make up a rhyme about the correct amounts.

 Take measuring cups and different-sized cartons to the sink and learn it by doing it.

 10 You have to memorize the Gettysburg Address. You practice by:

Writing it out until you can do it by memory.

Singing it until you can do it by memory.

 Acting it out with hand motions.

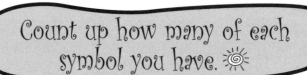

Count up how many of each symbol you have.

Many people learn in more than one way, so if you have some 👓 's, 👂 's, and 🤚 🤚 's, that's okay. The best way to learn something is to see it, hear it, and do it. But there is probably one way that is the best for you.

If you have mostly: ☀

'S YOU ARE A VISUAL LEARNER. That means you learn best when you see things. You would rather read a book than hear it read. Charts, graphs, maps, flashcards, and illustrations all help you when it's time to study. If you have to remember something, try drawing it or writing it out.

'S YOU ARE AN AUDITORY LEARNER. That means you learn best when you hear things. You would rather hear a story read to you than read it silently to yourself. Songs, rhymes, and saying things aloud help you when it's time to study. If you have to remember something, sing it to a tune you know, or rap it out.

'S YOU ARE A KINESTHETIC LEARNER. That means you learn best when you can do an experiment or activity, or when you can use your body to learn. You enjoy acting out a book as a play more than reading it or hearing it read. If you have to remember something, doing it will help you. You might use magnetic letters to practice your spelling words, or write them on paper then cut them up and put them back together like a puzzle.

Knowing your learning style can help you study better and remember more!

HOW YOU LEARN BEST applies to more than just school. It's also helpful when you want to memorize Scripture. Look at the ideas in "Try this" and use one of them to learn a new Bible verse this week.

 Pick three different ways to learn your spelling words (or something else that you have to memorize) this week. Try writing the words and erasing a letter at a time until you can spell them. Learn them by setting them to a tune, or try spelling them to a rhythm while bouncing a ball or jumping roping.

Are You Exercise Wise?

I praise you because I am fearfully and wonderfully made; your works are wonderful. I know that full well.

~Psalm 139:14

Holly grabbed her jump rope and went outside where four other girls were waiting with jump ropes. Holly joined them as they did stretches to warm up. She'd always thought jumping rope was just something the younger girls did on the playground at school. It wasn't something that interested her.

Then Holly and her friends watched a movie about a boy whose dad wanted him to be a boxer, but the boy had secretly joined a competition jump rope team. That was what the boy really wanted to do.

After Holly and her friends watched the movie, they decided to learn some of the moves and make up their own routine. After practicing for three months, they were getting pretty good. Plus Holly knew that jumping rope was better for her than sitting in the house watching television. She was having fun and exercising at the same time!

Quiz type: physical

Making exercise a part of your life is one of the best things you can do for your body. Exercise improves your health and keeps you fit. That's important because we all belong to God. He created us in an amazing and wonderful way, and it's our job to take care of the body He gave us. How much do you really know about exercise? Test your fitness knowledge with this quiz.

Circle true or false for each question below.

 If you exercise regularly you'll have more energy and less

body fat.
True   False

 Exercising only benefits your body and not your mind.
True   False

 Girls who are active in sports are less likely to use drugs.
True   False

 No pain, no gain is a true saying when it comes to exercise.
True   False

 Your body has about 100 muscles in it.
True   False

 Having gym class first thing in the morning is a bad way to

start the school day.
True   False

 Your muscles need oxygen to work.
True   False

8 Push-ups, chin-ups, and squats are all good ways to work your muscles.

True   False

9 You need to exercise at least an hour a day to make a difference in how fit you are right now.

True   False

10 You will stick with a fitness activity longer if it's a fun activity for you.

True   False

ANSWERS:

1 **True.** Exercise has a lot of benefits. Having more energy and less body fat are only two of them. Other benefits are stronger bones and joints, stronger muscles, and a stronger heart and lungs.

2 **False.** Exercise also helps relieve stress and work off anger or tension. It can boost your self-confidence and self esteem. It makes you feel better about your body.

3 **True.** Playing sports gives you a sense of belonging and self-esteem. Plus, athletes know that they need to take good care of their bodies. Unfortunately, some girls turn to drugs to find a sense of self-worth, but drugs (except the ones your doctor gives you) hurt, rather than help the body.

4. False. Activities like walking, dancing, riding your bike, skating, jumping rope, and throwing a Frisbee are all good exercises. In fact, if you exercise hard and long enough that you feel pain, you need to slow down.

5. False. Your body has about 650 muscles. They make up almost half of your weight. Try to do fitness activities that use a variety of muscles.

6. False. Gym class can energize you to face the school day by working off your tension and stress. Any activity works your muscles, including your heart. It makes your muscles use oxygen and brings fresh oxygen to the muscles as you use them. This helps start your day with you feeling alert and energized.

7. True. Exercise makes your muscles use oxygen. When you use those muscles for 15 minutes or more at a time, they need more oxygen to work their best. The more fit you are, the better your heart and lungs can pump oxygen-rich blood to your muscles. The more oxygen your muscles get, the better they work and the less tired you get.

8. True. To become stronger, your muscles need to meet resistance. This means that they need to push against something. When this happens, the muscles contract and become stronger. When you do push-ups, chin-ups, and squats, your own weight is the resistance.

9. False. Any amount of exercise done regularly will improve your fitness level. Even something such as climbing stairs every day instead of taking the elevator will improve your fitness level. If you aren't used to exercising, start with 20 minutes a day. Choose some activities from the "Try This" section. Be sure to talk with your parents, and possibly your doctor, before you start a fitness program. The key is to do a little bit every day.

10. True. If you're bored or not enjoying an activity, you probably won't stick with it. There are lots of fun ways to stay fit. Check out the choices in the "Try This" section and add some of your own!

How did you do?

8-10 EXERCISE WISE! You know what it takes to stay fit. Hopefully that means you exercise regularly. If not, choose one of the activities below and get started today!

5-7 YOU'RE ON YOUR WAY to learning what it takes to keep your body fit. Make sure you spend 30 minutes a day at least three days a week exercising. Just find an activity you enjoy and you'll look forward to your exercise times.

0-4 WHEW! Good thing you're reading about exercise and fitness! Find a friend to exercise with and it'll be more fun. Choose one of the activities below to do together.

JUST AS IT'S IMPORTANT to exercise our physical bodies, it's important to exercise our spirits, too. You can do this by reading your Bible, sharing a favorite verse with someone, or doing a good deed for someone to show how God's love shines through you!

Try this Get physical! Do one of these activities each day this week to stay fit. Put a check by each one you do!

____ **WALK TO SCHOOL** if you live close enough.

____ **INLINE-SKATE** around your neighborhood.

____ **BIKE** to your friend's house.

____ **TAKE THE STAIRS**, not the elevator.

____ **WALK YOUR DOG.**

____ **TAKE DANCE LESSONS** or invent a new dance.

____ **PLAY BASKETBALL** with a sibling or friend.

After you've checked off all of the activities on the previous page, write about it here!

How did it go? What was your favorite activity?

_____

_____

_____

_____

Is there another activity that might work better for you? Which one? Why?

_____

_____

_____

_____

_____

Quiz #13

What Does Your Room Reveal About You?

But everything should be done in a fitting and orderly way.

~1 Corinthians 14:40

Okay, to be honest, the verse on the previous page isn't talking about how you hang your clothes in your closet or arrange your school books on your desk. It's talking about how things should be done in a church service.

At the same time, God cares about every part of your life. He cares about how you do your jobs, the way in which you do your homework, and even how you clean your room (Colossians 3: 17,23). You might share a room with one or more sisters. In that case you may have to compromise about how your room is cleaned, organized, and decorated.

Quiz type: social/emotional

What's in your room and how it's arranged and organized can say a lot about you. Clear a spot on your bed or at your desk and see what this quiz reveals. If none of the answers really describe your room as it is, just pick the one you wish were true or would most likely be true.

1 You and your friends are going to do your homework together in your room. You:

A. Push enough junk off of your bed for all of your friends to sit down.

B. Have each of them get cozy with one of your oversized throw pillows.

C. Have your room so organized that everyone can have her own spot.

D. Hook your music player into a speaker dock for tunes to study by.

2 You're running late for school and still need to get your shoes. You:

A. Hope they are somewhere under the mound of clothes on your floor.

B. Grab them out of a decorated basket by the door.

C. Know they are right on your shoe rack where they belong.

D. Have to decide which of your shoes goes best with your outfit.

3 The most important thing in your room is:

A. Your bed, if you can locate it under the piles of clothes, books, and CDs piled on it.

B. The photos of your friends in coordinating pastel frames.

C. Your shelf of books arranged by authors' last name.

D. The posters of your favorite movie stars on your walls.

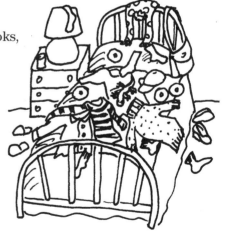

4 Mostly you use your room for:

A. Dropping off your stuff.

B. Hanging out.

C. Sleeping or studying.

D. Listening to music or watching TV.

5 You get to repaint your room. What color do you want it?

A. It's okay the way it is.

B. Pink, light blue, or yellow.

C. Plain white.

D. Anything bright or splashy.

6 What is most likely on your desk?

A. Every homework paper handed back this year, movie tickets, play programs, magazines, books, and trash.

B. Baskets holding pencils, pens, and other supplies, photos of friends, and a teddy bear your friend won for you at the fair.

C. Unfinished homework stacked in a pile, pens and pencils in holders, paper clips, rubber bands, and a dictionary—anything you might need to do your homework.

D. Lava lamp, photo of your favorite TV character, gel pens (one for every color in the rainbow), and a pile of CDs of the latest Christian bands.

7 You need to find your math book. Where is it?

A. Probably under the pile of clothes on your closet floor.

B. In your backpack hanging on the back of your door.

C. With your school supplies and other books stacked neatly on your desk.

D. On your bean bag chair.

8 The first thing people notice about your room is:

A. The dirty clothes on the floor.

B. Your collection of stuffed animals.

C. How organized it is.

D. The disco ball hanging in the middle of your room.

Count up how many A's, B's, C's, and D's you circled. ☀

If you have mostly:

�֎ **A'S DISASTER ZONE!** How do you find anything in your room? Wow! Clothes, papers, books, and shoes everywhere! You might want to organize a bit—throw out unrecognizable food, put clothes in the wash or on a hanger, and find a safe place for your school stuff. Try using large baskets—one for school supplies, one for books or collections, and so on. You are probably disorganized in other areas of your life, too. You may have trouble getting homework turned in on time and tasks done. Have a friend or a parent help you get organized and life will be easier for you.

☼ **B'S COZY AND COMFORTABLE.** Most of the stuff in your room is "cute." Things like stuffed animals, photos of friends, and keepsake items dominate your room. But be careful not to collect so much stuff that your room becomes cluttered! Your room is a fun and relaxed place to be. That's important to you because that's the kind of person you are. Friends like to be with you and enjoy being in your room.

🐱 **C'S HOME OFFICE.** Your room is super organized. You don't have trouble finding anything because everything is right where it belongs. You tend to keep a tight schedule and are a responsible and reliable person. Don't forget to just have fun, too. Think about brightening up your room with a colorful rug or pillows.

❀ **D'S MODERN MOODS.** You like bright colors and the latest fashions and fads. Your room reflects this by your choice of colors, posters, and decorations. Too much color and light will make it hard to relax, so don't go overboard. You have a strong personality and opinions. Be careful to consider what others want and like when it comes to making decisions.

YOUR BEDROOM TELLS PEOPLE

a lot about you—what your favorite colors are, what you like to do, and so on. Did you know that God has a room in His house for you? It's true! Read John 14 for details. What do you think your heavenly room will look like?

 Bedrooms are lots of fun. You can fix up your room with these inexpensive items. Add them to your Christmas or birthday list:

* **A COMFORTER** that sets the mood and color scheme for your room.

* **PILLOWS** in the accent color in your comforter. For instance, if your comforter is light blue with small lavender flowers, add some lavender throw pillows to your room.

* **A COLORFUL** waste basket. You can either buy a colored one or use stickers or stencils to decorate a white one.

✻ **PICTURES** of your friends in plastic frames in your accent color or an assortment of colors.

✻ **A BULLETIN BOARD** to hang your favorite mementos.

✻ **A MAGAZINE RACK** or CD rack that attaches to the wall.

✻ **A WALL CLOCK** that fits the mood of your room.

✻ **AN EXTRA SHELF** for pictures or trophies.

✻ **BEAN BAG CHAIR.**

✻ **ITEMS FOR YOUR WALL** that match your personality. You might want posters or perhaps a picture or rug that you made yourself. One wall might be dedicated to photos you took on vacation, or to your shell collection in display boxes. Avoid putting so much on your walls that they look cluttered.

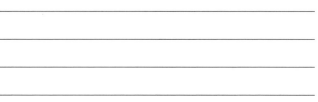

✻ **PLANTS, VASES,** candles, and other decorations for your desk or dresser top. Add your own ideas here:

_____

_____

_____

_____

Create your own adorable pillows to add color and personality to your room. Have fun!

You need:

* Hand towel in your favorite color (large enough to fold in half to make a pillow)
* Thread and needle or sewing machine
* Scissors
* Ribbons or buttons for decorations
* Polyester fiber fill (stuffing for the pillow)

To Make Pillows:

1. Fold towel in half
2. Choose how to decorate your pillow.

3. Sew buttons, ribbons and other decorations on one side of the towel. You can use fabric glue instead of sewing if you wish.

4. Sew around the outside edge of the pillow with the decorated side out. You can sew by hand or have an adult sew it on a sewing machine. Don't forget to leave a hole for the stuffing.

5. Stuff the pillow until it's as full as you want.

6. Sew the hole closed.

7. Use the pillow to decorate your room.

Quiz #14

How Do You Share Your Faith?

And you will be my witnesses in Jerusalem, and in all Judea and Samaria, and to the ends of the earth.

~Acts 1:8

Jesus told the early believers they were to share the Gospel message with others. Not all of them spread the Good News in the same way. Peter and Paul shared the Gospel by preaching to large crowds. Andrew and Philip talked to people one-on-one. Dorcas put her faith in action by reaching out to the needy. We don't all share our faith the same way today, either.

Jessica is a teen who loves to work with people. She shares her faith by going on student mission trips. She has been to New Mexico, and to Haiti several times. This year she is old enough to be a leader on a summer team that is going to Arizona.

Kristen is more of a one-on-one person. She looks around her middle school for girls who look lonely. She reaches out to them, and then invites them to her church.

Quiz type: Spiritual

Going on mission trips and talking to people one-on-one are only two ways to reach out to others. Take the quiz below to find out how you share your faith.

Start with the first list and check any of the statements that describe you. Go to the second list and do the same. Continue until you've read the sentences in all of the circles. If you have checked almost every statement in every circle, go back and make sure you only checked the ones that best describe you.

LiST

___ If someone is wrong, I tell him or her so.

___ If another student says something I disagree with, I offer him or her my opinion.

___ I love to give oral reports.

___ I like to lead group projects.

___ Teachers often ask me to be in charge of things.

LiST B

___ If someone is wrong, I explain why he or she is wrong.

___ I have a lot of patience.

___ I like to give explanations, like showing how something works for school reports.

___ I can easily organize projects.

___ Teachers ask me to explain the work to students who are having problems.

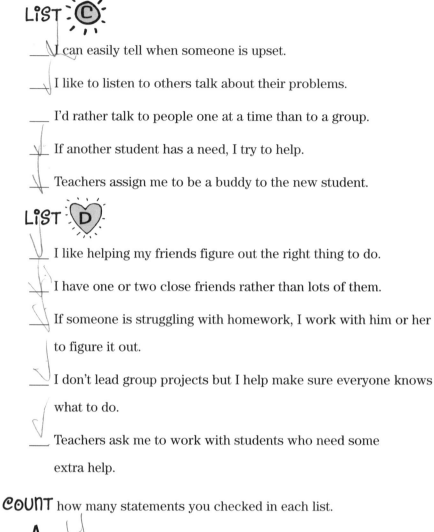

LIST **C**

____ I can easily tell when someone is upset.

____ I like to listen to others talk about their problems.

____ I'd rather talk to people one at a time than to a group.

____ If another student has a need, I try to help.

____ Teachers assign me to be a buddy to the new student.

LIST **D**

____ I like helping my friends figure out the right thing to do.

____ I have one or two close friends rather than lots of them.

____ If someone is struggling with homework, I work with him or her to figure it out.

____ I don't lead group projects but I help make sure everyone knows what to do.

____ Teachers ask me to work with students who need some extra help.

COUNT how many statements you checked in each list.

A: ____

B: ____

C: ____

D: ____

Which list has the most sentences checked?

Read the categorizations below to determine your witnessing style

a **YOU ARE An EVANGELiST.** Sharing your faith in front of people doesn't bother you. You know what you believe and are ready to tell whoever will listen. You are a leader, and people look up to you. While those are great qualities, be sure to think before you speak and consider other people's feelings. Not everyone is as outspoken as you are, but that doesn't mean that his or her opinion doesn't count. Work on being caring and compassionate.

B **YOU ARE A TEACHER.** Sharing your faith with others doesn't bother you, but you wouldn't just stand up in front of a group and talk. You use the Bible to teach others why you believe what you do. Explaining things to others is easy for you. It's important for you to have patience with those who can't explain their beliefs. Not everyone can share what he or she thinks in an organized manner.

C **YOU ARE A COMFORTER OR GiVER.** You share your faith with others who are upset or hurting inside. You have a tender heart and reach out to the person who is alone at recess or break time. Be sure to balance your caring, giving nature with common sense or you'll find yourself without paper, pencils, or lunch because you gave it all to someone you thought needed it more.

D YOU ARE A MENTOR.

You take people "under your wing" and help guide them. Rather than just presenting the Gospel to a friend, you would lead her to find Jesus for herself. And once she did, you would help her grow in her faith. Use that strength of gentleness to have patience with those who present the Gospel in a more outspoken way. Both ways are right!

GOD Connection

JESUS TOLD HIS DISCIPLES

to take the Gospel into the whole world, but he didn't assign them specific ways of doing it. God gave each of us unique ways of sharing our faith. And those ways will reach different people. Maybe one person will listen to the Gospel if it's presented in music. Maybe someone else will hear the Gospel if a friend sits next to him and shares it. Another person might believe in Jesus because someone did a kind deed for her.

Try this Share the Gospel in your own way with someone this week. Trust God to bring people to you who need to hear the Good News about Jesus. It's important to know that some people will not respond to the gospel, regardless of how it's communicated. It's the work of the Holy Spirit that converts people, not other human beings.

Three ways I can share the Gospel this week are:

1. _____

2. _____

3. _____

Quiz #15

Are You a Good Listener?

He who has ears, let him hear.

~Matthew 11:15

Jesus often spoke to large crowds of people.

Sometimes those people didn't really hear his message. They only heard what they wanted to hear. Jesus told them to use their ears and really listen to what he was telling them.

Quiz type: mental

During the day you spend a lot of time communicating—reading, talking, listening, or writing. Most of your time is spent listening, especially at school. You also have chances to hear God's Word in Sunday school and church. Listening skills are important! How do your listening skills stack up? Take the quiz below to find out.

Circle the answer that is most honest.

	A	B
1. When a friend is talking to me, I:	A. Concentrate on what he or she is saying.	B. Think about what I'm going to say next.
2. When my mom starts lecturing me about something I forgot to do, I:	A. Listen to find out what she wanted me to do and fix the problem.	B. Tune her out by thinking about what I'm going to do when she's done talking.
3. My history teacher is talking about causes of the war. I:	A. Listen to details but also try to see the big picture—the main idea.	B. Make sure I write down all the facts.
4. When a parent or friend is talking to me, I:	A. Listen to the words but also check out body language to get the true message.	B. Listen to the words. How can you tell what someone is thinking by the way they move and stand?
5. The pastor is preaching and there are too many words I don't understand. I:	A. Listen for things that I do understand.	B. Give up and decide the sermon is for the adults anyway.
6. A new girl approaches me in the hall and starts telling me how nervous she is about attending my school. I:	A. Make eye contact and nod to show I understand what she's saying.	B. Look around for my friends while I listen so they can join me.
7. When a friend is telling me about a problem, I:	A. Listen to her words but also try to figure out what she really means.	B. Listen to what she is saying and hope she is saying what she really means.
8. My friend keeps talking on and on about a fight with her mom. I:	A. Wait for a pause in her story and then tell her she really needs to talk to her mom about it.	B. Interrupt her story to tell her about my own fight my mom, which was so much worse.

How did you do?

In each situation, the "A" column is the situation where you would be a good listener.

6-8 A'S: YOU'RE TUNED IN. People probably enjoy talking to you because they can tell you are listening.

4-5 A'S: YOU'RE ON THE RIGHT TRACK, but you need to concentrate more on the person who is talking and less on yourself or what is going on around you.

0-3 A'S: YOU MIGHT FIND THAT PEOPLE DON'T TALK TO YOU as often as they do with their other friends. Make it a point to improve your listening skills and people will notice. They'll even seek you out when they need to talk.

Tune In!

Listen Up

✱ Since you can listen faster than someone can talk, use that time to think about what the person talking to you is really saying. Try it in school when your teachers are talking, and you might find it helps you remember things longer.

✱ Listen to your parents, teachers, or friends even if you aren't interested in what they're saying. You'd want them to do the same for you.

✱ Check out a person's body language while you're listening. Sometimes the way a person stands or gestures can tell you how she is really feeling. Look at your friend's facial expressions while she is talking.

✱ Make eye contact most of the time. If someone is talking and you are constantly glancing around to see who's walking by in the school hallway or what else is going on, that tells the other person you aren't that interested in what they are saying.

✱ If you need to interrupt, say, "Excuse me." Then wait for your friend to stop before you speak.

 The next time someone talks to you, look at that person and concentrate on what he or she is saying, not what you want to say next. Nod or smile to show you are really listening to them.

Pick one of the "Tune In" tips to try this week. Write it here:

_____

_____

How can you put it in practice this week?

_____

_____

 JUST AS YOU LISTEN TO YOUR PARENTS AND TEACHERS, it's important to listen to God. You do this when you read His Word and let the message reach your heart. You listen to God when you pay attention to what your Sunday school teacher and pastor say each week. What other ways can you listen to God?

Quiz #16

Are You Crazy for Clothes?

Therefore, as God's chosen people, holy and dearly loved,
clothe yourselves with compassion, kindness,
humility, gentleness and patience.

~Colossians 3:12

How does God say to clothe ourselves? With five positive character traits—compassion, kindness, humility, gentleness, and patience. These inward characteristics are more important than outward clothing. Does that mean it's wrong to think about styles and trends? No, just that who you are in your heart is more important than what you wear.

Quiz type: physical

How much do clothes mean to you? Do you like to have the latest styles or your old favorites? Are new clothes a priority or a pain? Take the quiz below to find out where you stand when it comes to fashion.

1 You and your friends go to a new store. The clothing section:

A. Is the place you go to after you visit your favorite departments.

B. Is the place you head to first.

C. Is the place you avoid.

2 Your mom says you need an Easter outfit. You say:

A. "Can we do it after my favorite show?"

B. "Let's go!"

C. "You pick out something for me."

3 Your idea of shopping for back-to-school clothes is:

A. Getting a comfortable outfit or two.

B. Searching for the perfect outfit for the first day.

C. Making sure you have underwear without holes in it.

4 To you, the words "shoes to match your outfit" means:

A. Just making sure the colors don't clash.

B. Finding the best style and color.

C. Tennis shoes.

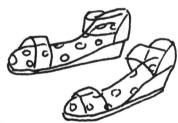

5 Getting dressed up for a party means:

A. Changing into your best jeans and shirt.

B. Choosing your most trendy outfit.

C. Your sweatpants aren't too dirty.

Count up how many A's, B's, C's, and D's you circled.

MOSTLY A'S: Clothes aren't the most important thing in your life. You do give some thought to what you wear, but you don't get too worried about it. As long as your clothes are comfortable and match, you're ready to go.

MOSTLY B'S: Clothes are important to you. You enjoy having the latest styles and looking your best. Shopping for clothes isn't a chore; it's one of your favorite things to do! Make sure you don't get too fashion obsessed or you won't have time for more important things like God and friends.

MOSTLY C'S: You tend to be fashion-challenged. You grab the first clean thing out of your closet or off the floor each morning for school. You'd be happy never to dress up or shop for clothes. You might want to give a little more thought to your clothes. After all, there are more options than just sweatpants and jeans.

Even if you aren't that concerned about the latest fashions, you want to look the best you can without trying to be someone you're not. After all, your clothes are a reflection of the person you are inside.

THIS WEEK BE SURE to clothe yourself with compassion, kindness, humility, gentleness, and patience with the same care—or more—that you give to clothing your body. Find one way each day to show each of these five characteristics.

Look through your closet. Are there clothes that you haven't worn for a while? Try mixing and matching some of your favorites with the pieces that you don't wear as much. Energize the outfit with a cute accessory. If you are fashioned challenged, ask a friend to come over and help you pick out pieces that look good together and find a way to add some pizzazz.

Holy Outfit Puzzle

Arrange the given words so they fit into the boxes below in order to find out how God dresses you every single day! Hint: All words will be used only once.

Isaiah   righteousness   me

garments   robe   clothed

salvation

For he has ⬚⬚⬚⬚⬚⬚⬚ me

with ⬚⬚⬚⬚⬚⬚⬚⬚ of

⬚⬚⬚⬚⬚⬚⬚⬚⬚ and

arrayed ⬚⬚ in a ⬚⬚⬚⬚

of ⬚⬚⬚⬚⬚⬚⬚⬚⬚⬚⬚⬚⬚

~ ⬚⬚⬚⬚⬚⬚ 61:10

Puzzle answer at the back of the book.

Quiz #17

How Content Are You?

For I have learned to be content whatever the circumstances.

~Philippians 4:11

Kenzie looked at the box sitting on the table. It was wrapped

in bright paper. Today was her twelfth birthday, and her grandmother had brought the present earlier in the day. Kenzie hoped there was something really awesome in that box.

It wasn't that Kenzie was unhappy with the things she owned, it was just that she had so much less than her friends. Most of them had their own cell phones, digital music players, and laptop computers.

Kenzie picked up the box. It was heavy. She wondered if it could be a laptop. She didn't know if her grandmother even knew what a computer was, so Kenzie wasn't going to get her hopes up. She sat the box next to a smaller one that was sure to hold jewelry and a flat box that probably contained clothing.

Finally it was time to open presents. Kenzie opened the smaller boxes first. The jewelry box held a necklace with her name on it, and the clothing box held a new jacket she'd wanted. Slowly Kenzie picked up the box from her grandmother and opened it.

Kenzie stared at the present. It was a thick binder with little cartoon bunnies on it. It would have been the perfect present if she was six, but she was twelve! Kenzie wasn't sure what to do. She smiled weakly at her grandmother and managed to say, "Thank you."

Quiz type: social/emotional

Being content means accepting things the way they are, even when you don't get your own way, and being thankful for what you have rather than complaining about what you don't have. Sometimes it's hard to be content! How well do you do? Take the quiz below to find out.

1 You want to go to summer camp with your friends, but there just isn't money for you to go. Your dad says he will take you on an overnight campout instead. **You:**

A. Tell him if you can't go to camp you won't go anywhere.

B. Tell him you'd love to camp out with him, and that you hope you'll be able to go to camp next year.

C. Complain that you'd rather go to camp, but if the campout is all he has to offer you'll take it.

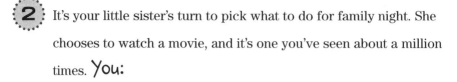

2 It's your little sister's turn to pick what to do for family night. She chooses to watch a movie, and it's one you've seen about a million times. You:

A. Tell your sister that you'll scream if you have to watch that movie one more time.

B. Understand that it's her favorite movie and you will get to choose the activity next week.

C. Watch the movie with a lot of moaning and groaning.

3 You try out for the school play. Instead of getting the speaking role you wanted, you are chosen to sing in the chorus. You:

A. Tell the director that if you can't have a speaking part you don't want to spend the time at play practice.

B. Decide to do your best in chorus so that you can feel like an important part of the play.

C. Tell your friends you'll be in the chorus, but you know you'd be better at the speaking part than the girl who got it.

Instead of your dream vacation to the big amusement park, you're at a cabin on a little lake. **You:**

A. Sit inside, refuse to take part in any activities, and remind everyone that you wanted to go to the amusement park.

B. Decide to find out what there is to do so your family can enjoy the lake vacation.

C. Take part in activities but complain that the spinning teacups would be much more interesting.

5 Your friend asks you to her fabulous birthday sleepover, but your family is going to your grandmother's house that same weekend. Your parents promise that you can have some friends over for pizza the next weekend. **You:**

A. Cry and beg your parents to change the visit to grandmother's house. If that doesn't work, scream that life really isn't fair, you never get your own way, and that you hate pizza.

B. Tell your friend that you are disappointed, but that you hope she and the others will come to your house for pizza the next weekend.

C. Make sure everyone in the car is as miserable as you are and tell your parents that they'd better get really good pizza for your party.

Count how many you have of each letter.

GIVE YOURSELF 0 points for every **A** you circled. Give yourself 2 points for every **B** you circled. Give yourself 1 point for every **C** you circled. Total your points.

0-4 POINTS: You are not content. When things get tough or you don't get your own way, you pout or whine or refuse to take part in an activity. Really, you are the one missing out. Stop, sit down, and make a list of 10 blessings in your life. If you can't think of 10, it's time to think hard about your life. Ask God to open your heart and your eyes to all of the things He's provided as a blessing to you. Try to think more about the things you are thankful for than the things you don't have.

5-7 POINTS: You accept things the way they are, but you are unhappy about it. You often make those around you unhappy. Try to accept disappointments and unwanted situations with a good attitude. This will make you and those around you happier. You'll be much more fun to be with.

8-10 POINTS: You are content with your life. You face disappointments with a good spirit and try to make the best of unpleasant situations. You aren't jealous when others get what you want, and you aren't angry when you don't get your own way. Your good attitude makes you like a light shining out Jesus' love.

 **THE WAY TO BE CONTENT** is to be thankful for what you have. Focus on the things you do have rather than on what you don't have. Do you have food and clothing (even if it's not "the right" brand)? You probably take those things for granted, but people in some countries don't have food or clothing. Sometimes they go days without food at all or have only a few bites to eat. Do you have safe water to drink and medicine to take or a doctor to visit when you're sick? Not everyone has those things. People die from lack of safe water or medicine to cure an infection or disease.

When you're feeling unhappy about your possessions, take a look at many people in third world countries—or even some people in our own country—and be thankful for having what you need.

Try this The key to contentment is to be thankful for what you do have. Take time this week to thank the people who give you what you need or do things to help you. Write a note thanking your mom for fixing your favorite foods or your dad for helping you with math. Write a thank-you note to the bus driver, cafeteria worker, custodian and others who do things for you.

I will write a note to these three people this week:

1. _____

2. _____

3. _____

Make It

Here's an easy card you can make to write the thank-you notes.

You Need:

* Piece of heavy paper in a rectangular shape
* Craft foam in your choice of color
* Stiff paint brush—stencil brush is best
* Paint—use a color that will coordinate with the craft foam
* Green puff paint (or marker)
* Button or pompon for flower center

To Make Notes:

1. Fold the paper in half to make a card.

2. Cut a flower pot shape from craft foam.

3. Draw a stem and leaf with the puff paint or with a green marker.

4. Trace the flower pattern (below) onto another piece of paper. Cut it out. The paper with the flower cut out is your stencil pattern.

5. When the paint is dry, position the pattern where the flower would go.

6. Dip your brush into the paint and tap it on paper to get off any extra. Brush inside the stencil pattern to make your flower.

7. Allow it to dry.

8. Add a button or pompon for the flower center.

9. Make as many cards as you want to write thank you notes this week.

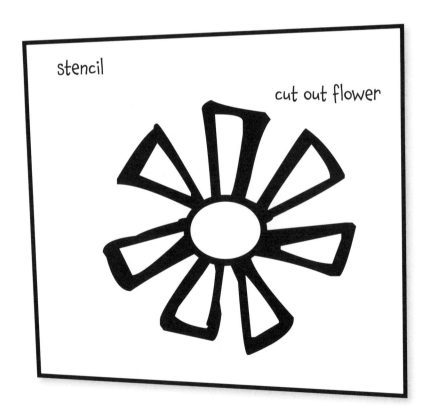

stencil

cut out flower

Quiz #18

Does Your Life Point to God?

Therefore, if anyone is in Christ, he is a new creation;
the old has gone, the new has come!

~2 Corinthians 5:17

"Come on," Lauren said. "Hurry up or the other teams will collect more canned food than we do." Lauren, along with Hailey and Mallory, pulled their wagon up to the next house.

Hailey knocked on the door. When a man opened it, Hailey explained that the sixth grade Sunday school classes were collecting canned food for the church food pantry. The church gave the food to families who were too poor to buy any.

The man walked away from the door and returned a few minutes later with four cans of soup. "Thank you," Hailey said. She put the cans in the wagon with the rest of the food they'd collected.

Lauren, Hailey, and Mallory collected food from four more houses. Then it was time to meet back at the van. The girls unloaded the cans into boxes labeled with their teacher's name. Whichever class had collected the most boxes of food would get a pizza party after church Sunday.

Lauren hoped her class got the pizza party, but most of all she hoped that the food would be given to the families who needed it most.

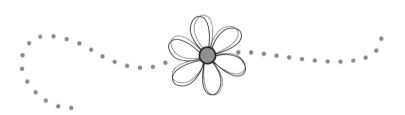

Quiz type: spiritual

Our good works don't make us right with God. Only Jesus can do that. But the way we live our lives shows that God's spirit is working in us. Does your life point to God? Take the quiz below to find out. Choose the answer that best describes what you would honestly do.

 You are sitting with your two best friends in Sunday school when a new girl walks in. She looks nervous, and she's not really dressed the same as everyone else. You:

A. Clear off a chair for her and keep talking to your friends.

B. Hope someone else talks to her.

C. Ask her to join you and your friends.

2 Your mom is out of town. Your dad comes home from work, drops into a chair, and flips on the television. You're hungry! You:

A. Cook something for yourself to eat.

B. Cook something for both yourself and your dad.

C. Beg your dad to order pizza for both of you.

3. You walk by your baby brother and realize he really needs a new diaper! **You:**

A. Change the diaper so he'll feel better and you can breathe.

B. Take your brother along with a diaper and wipes to your mom.

C. Ignore it and hope someone else discovers it.

 4. You are headed to your friend's house to shoot baskets when you see your elderly neighbor struggling to rake his yard. **You:**

A. Feel grateful you don't have that many trees in your yard!

B. Tell him you're going to a friend's house, but you'll help him if he's not done by the time you're done playing.

C. Go get your friend and rake the yard together because you can do it much easier and faster than your neighbor can.

5. You arrive home from school and find trash all over the yard. Your mom took the trash out before she left for work and must not have put the lid on tightly. Your dog has ripped up the bag and spread the trash everywhere. **You:**

A. Clean it up. You should have taken out the trash for your mom anyway.

B. Leave it until your mom gets home so she can see what happened.

C. Clean it up and hint that you could really use a bigger allowance.

6 The Sunday school lesson is about "God loves a cheerful giver." You remember that you received a lot of money for your birthday and the money is still in your dresser drawer. You:

A. Figure out what your tithe (10%) would be and put it in the offering the next week.

B. Give a generous Easter offering in addition to your tithe.

C. Leave it in you drawer so you'll have spending money for vacation this summer.

 7 You win a Bible for saying the most Bible verses during the quarter. You already have a Bible. You:

A. Give it to a kid who rides the bus to church and doesn't have a Bible.

B. Give your old one to the kid who doesn't have a Bible.

C. Keep it—he could have learned the verses if he wanted the Bible.

8 The boy who sits behind you at school asks if he can borrow a pencil. You know he doesn't really mean borrow because he's "borrowed" at least four pencils so far that you haven't gotten back. You:

A. Lend him the pencil and remind him to bring his own the next day so he can return yours.

B. Tell him to bring his own because you aren't a school supply store.

C. Give him a ratty old one that he can keep.

9 Your little sister asks you to read her a book. You don't have anything else to do, but reading to her isn't on your "favorite activities" list. **You:**

A. Pick the shortest book and read it to her.

B. Read her your old favorites.

C. Tell her to ask your dad to read to her.

 10 Your school is collecting baby clothes for the pregnancy center. **You:**

A. Decide not to bother with it.

B. Ask your mom to buy you baby clothes to donate.

C. Use your allowance and buy a cute baby outfit.

Check your answers here and see how many points you get for each question.

Points: Your points for each question:

1.　A. 1 point　　B. 0 points　　C. 2 points _____

2.　A. 0 points　　B. 2 points　　C. 1 point _____

3.　A. 2 points　　B. 1 point　　C. 0 points _____

4.　A. 0 points　　B. 1 point　　C. 2 points _____

5.   A. 2 points   B. 0 points   C. 1 point _____

6.   A. 1 point   B. 2 points   C. 0 points _____

7.   A. 2 points   B. 1 point   C. 0 points _____

8.   A. 2 points   B. 0 points   C. 1 point _____

9.   A. 1 point   B. 2 points   C. 0 points _____

10.   A. 0 points   B. 1 point   C. 2 points _____

Total points: _____

How did you do?

15-20 POINTS, SUPER! You are obeying the Lord in doing good to others. Your works show that God is working in you.

10-14 POINTS, GOOD JOB. You are thinking about your choices and trying to make the right ones. If you aren't sure what to do, ask God for help in making the best choices.

5-9 POINTS, SO-SO. You sometimes remember to do good to others, but many times you do what is best for you. Ask God to help you put others first from now on.

LESS THAN 5, UH-OH. Time to get serious about talking with God about doing good works.

THE THINGS YOU DO EACH DAY show others what is in your heart. Matthew 7 says that you are known by your fruit. What kind of fruit are you bearing? Read Galatians 5:22-23 to see the fruit that God wants in your life.

You've heard people talk about doing one good deed a day. Not many people do that, but it's a good habit to start. Check which of these you can do this week.

___ Do a chore around the house when it's not your turn.

___ Make breakfast for your mom or dad.

___ Play a game with a younger sibling.

___ Make a cheerful card for a family member, teacher, or

Quiz #19

How Do You Handle Pressure?

Come with me by yourselves to a
quiet place and get some rest.

~Mark 6:31

Jesus' disciples had been busy teaching, preaching and healing others. They were tired and needed a break. Jesus saw the stress in their lives and invited them to join Him for some time to relax. Do you need to do the same?

You have homework that's due. Your parents expect you to help at home. You have after school band or cheerleading practice, and Bible verses to learn for church on Sunday. On top of all that, your science teacher has just announced that everyone must turn in a project for the science fair. Sometimes it seems there is just too much to do! That makes you stress out. You may also feel pressured when you're facing new or difficult situations.

Quiz type: mental

The pressure's on! How do you handle it? Take the quiz below and find out which breakfast cereal you are most like when it comes to handling stress.

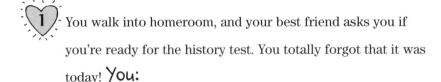

1 You walk into homeroom, and your best friend asks you if you're ready for the history test. You totally forgot that it was today! You:

A. Don't worry about it. You listened in class and reviewed your notes every night. You'll do okay even without cramming for it.

B. Totally panic! How could you have forgotten something so important?

C. Pretend you're sick and call your mom to take you home.

D. Ask your friend to quickly quiz you on the material.

2 This is the last week to read books for points in the classroom contest. You and another girl are tied for first place. You want to beat her because she wins at everything! You:

A. Read quickly but carefully to get as many additional points as possible.

B. See her checking out 10 new books and freak out. There's no way you can read that many!

C. Skim the books and hope the teacher doesn't ask you any questions about what you've read.

D. Find out what books your friends are reading and get together with them to read.

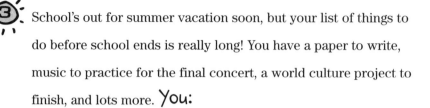 School's out for summer vacation soon, but your list of things to do before school ends is really long! You have a paper to write, music to practice for the final concert, a world culture project to finish, and lots more. You:

A. Make a list of everything you have to do, putting the most important things at the top. Then break each task into smaller parts you know you can accomplish.

B. Know you'll never get it done. Just hang on until summer and forget it all.

C. Talk your brother into doing half of it. If that doesn't work, pay him to do it.

D. Ask your friends over for a work night. Doing it together is more fun.

You're at summer camp. It's swim test time! All your friends are good swimmers, but you're not sure you even want to get into the water. You:

A. Decide you may as well give it a try. The worst thing that will happen is that you have to stay in the shallow end of the pool.

B. Run screaming toward the pool. Plug your nose and jump in. Hopefully someone will pull you out if you sink!

C. Fake it by "swimming" with your feet touching the bottom.

D. Ask if you can take the swim test with a friend. You may feel more confident with someone else with you.

5 You are meeting a cousin for the first time. Her mom writes to your mom every Christmas to brag about all your cousin's accomplishments and talents. You aren't sure you want to meet this wonder-cousin. **You:**

A. Remember that there are lots of things that you are good at also, and that God has a special plan just for you.

B. Ask yourself if it's too late to learn to play an instrument, try out for a play, and join the track team.

C. Stretch the truth about your accomplishments so you sound more talented than you are.

D. Ask if a friend can go along on the trip. If your cousin doesn't like you, you have your friend along for company.

How did you do?

🌼 **MOSTLY A'S: YOU'RE LIKE CHEERIOS.** You're steady and consistent. You face pressure confidently because you are prepared and ready. Things don't pile up at the last minute. You start projects early. You study every day instead of at the last minute. You probably find yourself frustrated with friends who don't plan ahead like you do. Try to be patient and

understanding. Encourage them to study with you each day after school or to go to the library and use the computers to start reports early.

☼ MOSTLY B'S: YOU'RE LIKE RICE KRISPIES.

When the pressure is on you snap, crackle, and pop! You forget about homework that is due and neglect to study ahead for tests. The night before your science project needs to be turned in, you beg your dad to help you build a model of the solar system. Save yourself some stress by planning ahead. Buy a calendar and write down when homework, projects, and papers are due. Start your project the first day and do a little each day until you're done. Make sure you don't plan to do more than you have time to do. Say "no" to things that don't interest you as much so that you'll have enough time to do what you really want.

♡ MOSTLY C'S: YOU'RE LIKE TRIX—OR ACTUALLY LIKE THE RABBIT who tries to get Trix by

pretending he's a kid. Rather than face the problem and look for a solution, you look for a way around it. Sometimes you can talk a sibling or friend into taking some of your responsibilities. Other times you try to talk your way out of completing projects and tasks or pretend to be sick to avoid the situation. You're developing some poor coping skills. Pray and ask God to help you take responsibility for the things that you need to do. Ask a parent to help you get organized and show you how to plan ahead and prepare. Then you won't need to look for a way out.

❀ MOSTLY D'S: YOU'RE LIKE LUCKY CHARMS.

Your friends are the marshmallows that give life a touch of sweetness. You depend on friends when you're feeling stressed. There's nothing wrong with getting support and help from friends, but be sure that you don't become too dependent on them. They are girls just like you and are facing pressures, too. Work on handling some of your problems alone. Help a friend instead of asking for help.

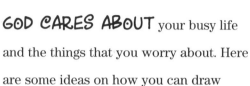

GOD Connection

GOD CARES ABOUT your busy life and the things that you worry about. Here are some ideas on how you can draw close to Him, even when you are under pressure!

* WRITE IT OUT. Keep a journal of your feelings. Later, you can look back and see how far you've come in your relationship with God.

* TALK IT OUT. Find a trusted adult or a mature friend. Tell that person whether you want advice or just want them to listen. Ask them to say a prayer for you.

* WALK IT OUT. Go for a walk or jog. Use your eyes to see God's creation. Use your ears to hear the world around you. Be aware of how big and wonderful God's creation is.

* FUEL UP! Fill your heart with God's Word and your body with high energy, nutritious food.

Low-Stress Puzzle

God's Word gives some good advice on how to handle stress. Use the box code below to help you decode the verse.

	✿	♡	◎	☆
1	a	b	c	e
2	f	h	i	l
3	m	n	o	r
4	s	t	u	x
5	y	d	p	g

Look under the first blank, at 1◎. To decode this, put one finger on the 1 and one on the ◎. Bring your fingers together until you touch "c." Write "c" on the line. Continue doing this until you can read the verse.

___ ___ ___ ___   ___ ___ ___   ___ ___ ___ ___
1◎ 1✿ 4✿ 4♡   1✿ 2☆ 2☆   5✿ 3◎ 4◎ 3☆

___ ___ ___ ___ ___ ___ ___   ___ ___   ___ ___ ___
1✿ 3♡ 4☆ 2◎ 1☆ 4♡ 5✿   3◎ 3♡   2♡ 2◎ 3✿

166

___ ___ ___ ___ ___ ___ ___   ___ ___
1♡ 1☆ 1◎ 1❀ 4◎ 4❀ 1☆   2♡ 1☆

___ ___ ___ ___ ___ ___ ___ ___   ___ ___ ___ .
1◎ 1❀ 3☆ 1☆ 4❀ 2❀ 3◎ 3☆   5❀ 3◎ 4◎

~1 Peter 5:7

Puzzle answer at the end of the book.

How can the advice in this verse help you cope with the stressful situations in your life?

_____

_____

_____

 Set aside 15 minutes a day to spend by yourself. Use the time to do one of the activities below or another activity that you like. Make sure whatever you do is relaxing, not a task you have to get done.

* Pray
* Keep a journal
* Write a poem
* Read a book
* Reread your favorite Bible story
* Write to a grandparent
* Listen to music
* Daydream!

Quiz #20

Which Activities are Right for You?

I press on toward the goal to win the prize for which God has called me heavenward in Christ Jesus.

~Philippians 3:14

The Apostle Paul writes about the Christian life as though it were a race. He talks about throwing off anything that might hold him back as he races toward the prize. Paul must have been familiar with physical exercise to use it as an illustration more than once in his letters. He knew his Christian faith was the most important part of his life, but he also knew that a full life involved plenty of exercise from engaging in fun and competitive activities.

Quiz type: physical

Whether you are already involved in sports or not, the activity below can help you choose a sport or physical activity you might enjoy.

Begin with the box marked "Start" and follow the path by choosing the sentences that best describe you.

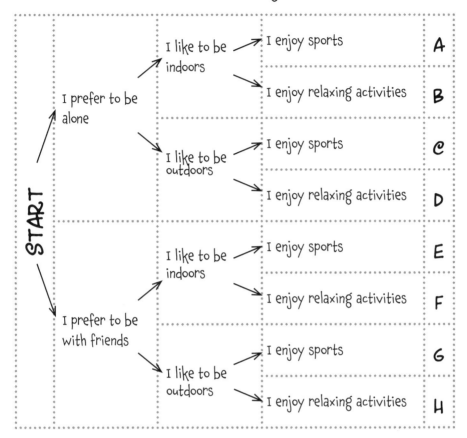

A. You like working out indoors and you prefer to do it alone. You might enjoy swimming laps at an indoor pool, running on an indoor track, climbing an indoor climbing wall, jumping rope, or learning to play racquetball.

B. You don't really enjoy physical activities. You prefer to do other kinds of activities by yourself indoors. Still, physical activity is good for you, so it's important to find something you like to do. You might want to get an exercise video and work out with it. You could also jump rope or dance to your favorite songs. You might enjoy swimming laps at an indoor pool or taking a karate class and practicing at home.

C. You enjoy physical activities you can do alone. You don't mind working your muscles hard, especially if you can be outdoors. There are lots of activities to do outside that will keep you fit while having fun. You might enjoy in-line skating, jogging, or swimming. You can also bike, cross-country ski, skateboard, or snowboard.

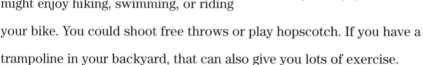

D. You don't really enjoy sports as much as other girls. But you do like doing things outdoors by yourself. You might enjoy hiking, swimming, or riding your bike. You could shoot free throws or play hopscotch. If you have a trampoline in your backyard, that can also give you lots of exercise.

E. You enjoy physical activities and would rather do them with a friend. You prefer indoor activities. There are many to choose from. You can play basketball, dodge ball, indoor soccer, or kickball. You might want to join a karate class with your friends and practice at home together. And just for fun you can try a game like Twister that uses physical skills.

F. You enjoy doing easy activities with your friends indoors. You might enjoy games such as badminton, volleyball, or ping-pong that require less running and jumping than basketball or kickball. Skating and bowling are fun activities you can do with your friends that will use your muscles and keep you moving.

6. You like most sports, especially the ones you can do outdoors with your friends. You can ride bikes or skate together. You might jog around the park or play basketball on the outdoor court. Baseball or soccer are also fun sports to do with friends outdoors. There are also all kinds of games you can play in a pool like tag, volleyball, or relays.

H. You aren't really into exercise, but you do like being outdoors with your friends. You might enjoy playing games or exercising together in a pool. You could also toss a Frisbee, or ride your bikes to the park. Try to do things that involve moving around and using your muscles rather than just sitting.

1 CORINTHIANS 6:19-20 says that our bodies are temples of the Holy Spirit and we should honor God with our bodies. That doesn't mean we have to be super athletes, but we can take time each day to give our bodies the exercise they need.

 Whether you consider yourself athletic or not, you can probably find at least one sport you enjoy whether it's running, dancing to your favorite CD, inline skating, or horseback riding. Invite a friend over this weekend to try several activities until you find one you both like.

What two activities can you try either alone or with a friend?

1. _____

_____

2. _____

_____

Quiz #21

Are You a Good Sport?

Whatever your hand finds to do, do it with all your might.

~Ecclesiastes 9:10

Megan walked into the dug out and pulled off her catcher's mask. She wanted to throw it on the ground but knew that wouldn't be good sportsmanship. It was hard to be a good sport when her softball team had lost every game. The problem wasn't that they weren't a good team, the real problem was that the pitcher and first baseman didn't like each other. Instead of working together to get players out at first, they ignored each other or blamed each other for mistakes. Megan wished one of them would drop off the team or that coach would bench them. Then maybe they could win a game.

Quiz type:
social/emotional

It's fun to win and it's not much fun to lose! However, it's important for you to be gracious in both victory and defeat. It's all about attitude. The key is to have a good attitude at all times no matter what happens. How well do you do at that? Take the quiz below to find out. Read each question and then color the shape in front of the answer that sounds most like what you would do.

1 Middle school cheerleading tryouts are taking place. It's your turn and you're doing great. Just as you do your final jump, your foot slips and you fall. What do you do?

○ Get up, smile, and finish.

☐ Blame whoever was supposed to clean the floor.

△ Leave the floor and hope the judges liked the rest of your routine.

176

2 You arrive early at the science fair and discover that you won the grand prize. Then you notice that the girl who always teases you for being slowest in PE didn't place at all. What do you do when she walks in?

◯ Find one good thing about her project to compliment her for.

▢ Say, "Ha! You might be better in PE but I aced you in the science fair."

△ Ignore her and spend time with your friends, enjoying your moment of fame.

3 Your girls' basketball team is playing a team known for fouling. You've been elbowed several times. But then you come down from a rebound and hit one of their players in the head with your elbow. What do you say?

◯ "Oops, sorry."

▢ "Move next time."

△ Nothing.

4 You and another band member are playing a duet at the city competition. You don't place well. What do you say?

◯ Maybe if I practice more I'll do better next time.

▢ Maybe if you would have practiced we'd have done better.

△ I guess the judge thought we stunk.

5 You pride yourself on being a good writer. You place second in an essay contest. When you read the essay that beat yours what do you think?

○ That's a really well-written essay.

☐ Mine should have won.

△ I wish I had won.

How did you do?

○ IF YOU HAD MOSTLY CIRCLES, you are a good sport! You like to win, but you accept it when you lose. You try to congratulate the winner. And if you are the winner, you make sure to say something nice to the loser. Way to go!

☐ IF YOU HAD MOSTLY SQUARES, you need to practice your sportsmanship skills! We'd all like to win but that rarely happens. Don't blame others when you lose. Just determine to do better the next time. And when you win, do it graciously, not rudely. Real winners have good attitudes!

△ IF YOU HAD MOSTLY TRIANGLES, you aren't a poor sport, but you're not really a good sport, either. Go a step further and compliment the winner, or if you are the winner, say something nice to the loser. Win or lose, people will admire you if you show good sportsmanship.

Tune In!

How to win with a smile

✻ Take a look at what happened. Why did you lose? What could you do differently next time?

✻ Let go of unfair situations. If a referee really did make a bad call, there's nothing you can do about it. Let go of it.

✻ Don't blame yourself, others, or God. That really doesn't help. If it's your fault, put your energy into practicing rather than acting out. Forgive others and remember that God's ways are always best.

✻ Put it in perspective. Think about how important this is in the overall picture of your life. You'll be in school at least four to five more years. Maybe more. Does this one loss really matter that much? Will it change the rest of your life?

✻ No one likes to lose. But everyone does from time to time. Accept the outcome with a smile and move on.

GOD DOESN'T KEEP TRACK of victories and losses. What's important to God is that we do our best with what He gives us. We are successful when we do this. And being a winner in God's eyes is more important than any ribbon or trophy here on Earth.

 Make sure you demonstrate a good attitude even when you lose. Whether you lose the solo in the spring musical to another student, lose the spelling bee to the class brain, or lose at a game, make it a point to congratulate the winner. Speak an encouraging word to others who have lost also. Bad attitudes are contagious—but so are good ones.

Phone Puzzle

One way to be a good loser is to think about others above yourself. What does the verse below say about thinking of others? There are two numbers under each line. The first number tells you which button to use. The second number tells you which letter on that button to use. For example, 6.2 would be button 6, second letter: N.

Do __ __ __ __ __ __ __ out of __ __ __ __ __ __ __
   6.2 6.3 8.1 4.2 4.3 6.2 4.1   7.4 3.2 5.3 3.3 4.3 7.4 4.2

__ __ __ __ __ __ __ __ or __ __ __ __
2.1 6.1 2.2 4.3 8.1 4.3 6.3 6.2   8.3 2.1 4.3 6.2

__ __ __ __ __ __ __ ,   __ __ __ in
2.3 6.3 6.2 2.3 3.2 4.3 8.1   2.2 8.2 8.1

__ __ __ __ __ __ __ __ consider __ __ __ __ __ __
4.2 8.2 6.1 4.3 5.3 4.3 8.1 9.3   6.3 8.1 4.2 3.2 7.3 7.4

__ __ __ __ __ __ than __ __ __ __ __ __ __ __ __ __ __ .
2.2 3.2 8.1 8.1 3.2 7.3   9.3 6.3 8.2 7.3 7.4 3.2 5.3 8.3 3.2 7.4

~Philippians 2:3-4

Puzzle answer at the end of the book.

What does this verse mean for you personally?

_____

_____

_____

Can you think of a time when you were selfish
and later wished you'd acted differently?

_____

_____

_____

How can you practice the advice in this passage?

_____

_____

_____

Quiz #22

How Do You Serve God?

Always give yourself fully to the work of the Lord, because you know that your labor in the Lord is not in vain.

~1 Corinthians 15:58

Dorcas was a woman in the Bible who lived in the port town of Joppa. She was kind to others, especially the poor. One day Dorcas died, and the people were very sad. They sent for the Apostle Peter. When Peter got to the house, a crowd was gathered there. They showed Peter coats and other clothing Dorcas had made for them. Peter told everyone to leave the room. Then he raised Dorcas from the dead through God's power. The people were happy when they saw Dorcas was alive and well.

Dorcas served God by making coats and clothing for the poor. She used her talent for God. There are lots of different ways to serve God. The way you can best serve Him depends on your personality and talents.

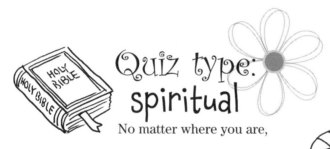

Quiz type: spiritual

No matter where you are, you can always find opportunities to serve God. Whether you're on family vacation, at church, at school, or hanging out with your friends you can always find fun activities to help others and let the light of God shine through you. Take the quiz below to find out how you can best serve God.

When it comes to spending time with people, I:

A. Think children are the most fun.

B. Want to help those who are poor or homeless.

C. Like to be with people my grandparents' age and older.

D. Would rather be by myself.

 I like to share my faith by:

A. Singing fun songs and doing activities.

B. Building churches or repairing campgrounds.

C. Talking to people who are lonely.

D. Sending postcards to people who have been absent from Sunday school.

 I can most imagine myself:

A. Holding little kids—even those who are sticky and dirty.

B. Digging and building.

C. Listening to other people tell their stories.

D. Working on a project alone or with a few friends.

4 People say I am:

A. Fun

B. Rugged

C. Compassionate

D. Motivated

5 I hope my activities this year include:

A. Playing, singing, telling stories, using puppets, and doing crafts.

B. Riding on a bus, pouring concrete, singing, meeting new people of all ages, and making friends with teammates.

C. Helping with household activities, listening to stories, sharing about my life, and helping with easy games and crafts.

D. Making phone calls, writing letters, handing out tracts, making posters, and organizing.

Count how many you have of each letter.

__A's   __B's   __C's   __D's

Don't worry if you have a mixture of letters. Read what all of the letters mean. You are probably interested in a few different ways to serve God. That just means more opportunities for you!

MOSTLY A'S. You have a heart for children your age and younger. You feel comfortable getting down on the floor with them to play or read a story. It'll probably be easy for you to share the good news about Jesus with the little ones through stories, songs, and games. Perhaps you can be a junior helper at Vacation Bible School this year. Don't overlook your own younger siblings. Make it a point to read a  Bible story or devotional with your younger brother or sister every day. Spend time with them, and you will be a big influence in their lives.

MOSTLY B'S. You love adventure and helping people who have less than you do. A short term mission program might be the ideal ministry for you. During that time you might build homes, perform puppet shows, sing, talk to people about Jesus, and even make some new friends. If you can't attend a program far from home, have your parents help you find out how you can get involved in your own town. Maybe your family could serve at a soup kitchen together, or you might be able to collect canned goods for a food bank or supplies for a center for young mothers. Don't forget to be a helper in your own home, too. Ask your mom or dad for suggestions on how you can make life easier for your own family.

MOSTLY C'S. Some people are uncomfortable around the elderly, but not you! This summer would be a great time to "adopt" an older person from your church as a grandparent. You could visit with them weekly. There are lots of things you could do to help them—mow their lawn, rake leaves, weed the garden, grab things that are hard for them to reach, and just be a listener and encourager. Some elderly people in nursing homes rarely get visitors, and you might just make their day. You could even make some special crafts to brighten up their rooms. Don't overlook your own elderly relatives. Write a letter to your great-grandmother or great-uncle. Be sure to write big and neat so it's easy to read. Send pictures, too.

MOSTLY D'S. You like to work behind the scenes, and your help is needed. Ask your pastor what you can do to help around the church. Perhaps you can organize the library or repair books. Maybe the nursery needs painting or the toys could use a cleaning. Maybe you could help out with a children's program. You might be able to help a busy mom by taking the children outside to play or reading to them. Don't forget to be a helper at home, too. See how many good deeds you can do this week without being detected!

GOD WANTS YOU TO SERVE Him, but He doesn't expect you to serve Him in the same way as your brother, sister, or even your best friend. God gave you a unique personality and your own set of talents and abilities. He wants you to use those to serve Him in your own special way.

 Don't wait until summer to get involved in serving God. Look around your church, school, home, and neighborhood. What can you do to help others? Write some of your ideas below, then talk to an adult about how to get started.

1. _____

2. _____

3. _____

4. _____

Make It

No matter how you choose to serve God, this cute flower pot pen holder can brighten up your desk and may even inspire you to write letters to those you care about!

You need:

* Ballpoint pen
* Green floral tape
* Scissors
* Silk or plastic flower with a metal stem
* Flower pot
* Paint in favorite color
* Paintbrush
* Craft foam
* Buttons or pompons for flower center
* Glue

To Make a Flower Pen:

1. Cut the stem of the flower to 3" long.

2. Remove the leaves from the stem.

3. Hold the stem along the pen tightly so that the flower lines up with the end of the pen.

4.   Wrap the length of the pen in floral tape. Be sure the tape secures the flower to the pen. Wrap the pen a second time if needed to secure the flower.

To Make the Pen Holder:

5.   Paint the flower pot. Let dry. Do this as many times as is needed to cover the pot.

6.   Cut flower shapes from the craft foam. You can cut two of different sizes and glue one on top of the other if you like. Make as many flowers as you'd like to decorate your pot.

7.   Glue a button or pompon in the center of each flower. Allow the flowers to dry.

8.   Glue the flowers to the pot. Allow to dry.

9.   Use the pot to hold your pens and other supplies.

Puzzle Answers

CH 1—PAGE 15

ANSWER: Before I formed you in the womb I knew you, before you were born I set you apart.

Jeremiah 1:5

CH 10—PAGE 92

ANSWER: Join with others in following my example, brothers, and take note of those who live according to the pattern we gave you.

Philippians 3:17

CH 16—PAGE 140

ANSWER: For he has clothed me with garments of salvation and arrayed me in a robe of righteousness.

Isaiah 61:10

CH 19—PAGE 166

ANSWER: Cast all your anxiety on him because he cares for you.

1 Peter 5:7

CH 21—PAGE 181

ANSWER: Do nothing out of selfish ambition or vain conceit, but in humility consider others better than yourselves.

Philippians 2:3-4